CHARLES EINSTEIN

How to Coach, Manage, and Play Little League Baseball

A COMMONSENSE INSTRUCTIONAL MANUAL

Foreword by WILLIE MAYS

A Fireside Book
Published by Simon & Schuster, Inc.
New York

THIS FIRESIDE EDITION, 1986
PUBLISHED BY SIMON & SCHUSTER, INC.
SIMON & SCHUSTER BUILDING
ROCKEFELLER CENTER
1230 AVENUE OF THE AMERICAS
NEW YORK, NEW YORK 10020
FIRESIDE AND COLOPHON ARE REGISTERED
TRADEMARKS OF SIMON & SCHUSTER, INC.
MANUFACTURED IN
THE UNITED STATES OF AMERICA
1   3   5   7   9   10   8   6   4   2

Library of Congress Cataloging in   Publication Data

Einstein, Charles.
How to coach, manage, & play Little League baseball.
Previously published as: How to coach, manage, and play
Little League baseball.
"A Fireside book."
Includes index.
1. Little League Baseball, inc. 2. Baseball for children. I. Title.
II. Title: How to coach, manage and play Little League baseball.
GV880.5.E57   1986   796.357'62   86-2052

ISBN: 0-671-20291-X

Contents

Foreword

When I was in military service we had a sergeant who was always saying there were four different ways of doing a thing: "The right way, the wrong way, the Army way, and my way."

From what I've seen, something like that is also true a lot of times when it comes to teaching baseball to Little Leaguers.

For instance, I've felt that when it comes to handling kids on the ball field, sometimes over-coaching is a lot worse than undercoaching.

A lot of other times, of course, there's more than one way to teach the same thing . . . and maybe more than one way for a boy to execute the same play, and still do it right.

Finally, there are some things that are just as well, at that age level, not being taught at all.

When I first met Charles Einstein in 1951, he was already a veteran baseball writer. He spent something like ten years, in New York, Arizona, and California, as a Little League manager, coach, and official. His own three sons each went through the whole span of Little League, from eight-year-old "peewees" to post-season all-star competition at the age of twelve.

So I think it is a good idea to have a book come along like this one which suggests some new ideas —at some places even a basic new approach— for teaching Little Leaguers, who now number in the millions.

But at the same time, to say that some of the things in this book are "new" is not to say that they haven't been tested out over years of direct first-hand experience on the author's part. So this book is on solid ground, and in reading it you will see that every time the author recommends something new or different, he also explains why. I think you'll agree the reasons make as much sense as the ideas themselves.

Willie Mays

[1]

Introductory

This book was undertaken in an effort to counteract some of the instructional problems that seem to have grown out of the very success of Little League baseball. This is not to say that other teaching materials do not exist. Indeed, the conscientious manager or coach in Little League today can find access to a near-bewildering arsenal of advice— some of it from his players. For it is worth noting that, as the Little Leagues have expanded since the war, so have the major leagues. Where once it was an exception to find a nine-year-old who had ever seen a Big League game, today's rarity, thanks to television and migration, is to find one who hasn't. Thus exposed, a youngster may acquire the notion that he knows more about baseball than his coach. Once in a while, he does.

Anyone who doubts that the growth of Little League has produced new headaches for the manager and coach should reflect that the game has

even gone so far as to invent its own disease—
"Little League elbow." What it has also produced,
with more serious consequences, is a generation of
players who have gone on into the ranks of professional baseball. A case in point would be that of
Ed Kranepool, of the New York Mets, who
solemnly listed his Little League team when asked
for evidence of his amateur experience.

Things like that can be regarded as critical, for
purposes of this book, because they symbolize the
extent to which Little League baseball has become
interchangeable with baseball itself. The more the
boys' game becomes synonymous with the men's
game, the further lost to view are the distinctions
between the two. Yet the more the Little League
coach fails to perceive these distinctions, the poorer
job he will do.

These differences come in three sizes, pertaining
to teacher, to pupil, and to the physical nature of
the game itself.

Perhaps the last of those three is most immediately
apparent. We know that when, over a century ago,
Abner Doubleday—or Alexander Cartwright—laid
out the first ball field, with 90 feet between bases,
he was creating (maybe unwittingly) a near-poetic
contest between man and ball. Paul Gallico cele-
brated this in his book, *Farewell to Sport:*

> The baseball diamond is no diamond at all, but
> actually a square set up on one of its points, and
> the bases, home to first, first to second, second to
> third, and third to home, are each exactly 90 feet
> apart. The pitcher's box is 60½ feet from home
> plate. The distance from home plate to second
> base, which is the line on which the catcher

10

throws in the attempt to catch a man who is stealing, is a fraction over 127 feet. And the entire
science and thrill of the American game of baseball, developed from an old English game called
rounders, lie tucked away in those measurements.
They are very rarely examined, and still more
rarely thought of, even by the players. Most of the
men who play the game haven't the vaguest notion
of the miracles of timing and precision they perform.

"Miracles" is a good word for it, and we can
readily see that if those 90-foot distances between
bases were extended by, say, 30 feet each—perhaps
to accommodate a race of giants—then the delicate
balance of offense versus defense, with those new
120-foot distances, would be ruined for good and
all.

To some extent, a Little League field imposes
that same kind of alteration upon the basic game,
only in reverse. Instead of adding 30 feet to the
distance between bases, Little League subtracts 30
feet.

It is a pretty fable that this reduction from 90 to
60 feet between bases results in a diamond two-
thirds regulation size, and that therefore Little
League is simply "baseball in miniature." There is
nothing "two-thirds" about it. With the 90-foot
distances, the square footage within the base lines
is 8,100 square feet. Using the 60-foot distances,
you get 3,600 square feet. Thus in truth a regulation infield is more than twice as large as a Little
League infield. Extend the foul lines to the fences,
and the typical regulation playing field, compared
with Little League, becomes *four times* as large!

There is nothing basically wrong—and a good deal basically right—in putting boys in the nine-to-twelve age group on a smaller field. But the wise manager and coach will want to bear in mind the two reasons why the smaller field was established.

Both reasons are eminently practical. The first of them, dealing with the square-footage factor mentioned above, made it possible to put four Little League fields in the space occupied by one regulation field. Nothing so stimulated the expansion of the Little League program as much as its relatively small demands for space; the basic requirement has been for one acre instead of four. In many places, indeed, Little League has simply staked out already-existing softball diamonds, which have the same dimensions.

The second reason, just as realistic as the first, is the fact that Little League pitchers can throw strikes with regularity from 46 feet. From 60½ feet, they cannot. It is this consideration, not the running distance between bases, which from the playing standpoint dictated Little League dimensions. And in so doing, it imposed a measure of artificiality upon the rest of the game. The extent of this artificiality often goes unnoticed, because small boys seem to have a way of fitting onto small fields. But anyone seeking visible evidence of the grief it can cause need only watch a Pony League game—an organized program for boys thirteen and fourteen, just out of Little League—where the base lines are neither 60 feet nor 90 feet, but just in between at 75 feet (once again basically out of consideration for the pitcher's control). In Pony League, unlike Little League, base runners are permitted to take a lead. With a lead and only 75 feet to go to begin with, it becomes literally impossible for a runner on second not to be able to steal third—unless the defending shortstop or second baseman actually stands on second base, thereby abandoning his normal fielding position, to hold him close. The lesson here exposes itself with dramatic clarity: you do not tamper with Abner Doubleday's (or Alexander Cartwright's?) distances without imposing important changes upon the game itself.

Why, then, can adults play softball on a diamond of Little League dimensions and create an exciting replica of baseball itself? The reason here is quite simple. When the Little League fathers decided to put their game on a softball-size diamond, they forgot to tell the ball. A Little League baseball is only a fraction smaller and lighter than a regulation hardball, and if the players perform like kids, which they are, it is of little help that the ball persists in behaving like an adult. In the shortened distance from home plate to outfield, it can and does sail through that infield in disparate proportion to the youthful defender's ability, however instinctive, to react. The hard line drive from the bat of a Little Leaguer will not travel so far, nor perhaps fly so high, as its counterpart from the bat of a professional. But with a third baseman playing 30 feet closer to home and standing a foot shorter in height, any theory of relativity ceases to exist. We all know the difference, but, to repeat, nobody told the ball. The regulation out becomes the Little League hit, and there is nothing anybody can do about it.

As noted before, the difference in size between Little League and regulation diamonds is apparent for all to see. More subtle, perhaps, are the basic reasons for that difference and some of the changes in conditions and techniques that must result. Directly affected, in many cases, is the tendency on the part of coaches to teach Big League tactics to Little League players. These days there are even "clinics," held by major leaguers and heavily attended by Little League coaches, designed to augment the coaches' comprehension of the finer points of baseball. Though well-conceived, such sessions tend to teach *baseball*, as opposed to *Little League baseball*. The discerning manager or coach, benefit though he may by attendance at such clinics, will remember not to confuse the two.

Let us take an example. There is a man on second, no one out, close game in an early inning. The hitter singles to right field. All basic teaching tells us to bring the first baseman into the play as cutoff man. He will take up a position fairly close to the pitcher's mound, in a line between the right fielder's throw and the catcher. If the man is going to score from second, he will cut off the throw, and by so doing keep the hitter from advancing to second on the play to the plate. If there is a play at home, he will let the throw go through to the catcher. This is the way they do it in the Big Leagues. Not only in the Big Leagues, but in the minors, in college, even in high school.

Yet, in Little League, the fact is that this is a bad play. And it is a bad play for no fewer than three very good reasons:

1. In the regulation game, a first baseman is used as a cutoff man on plays to the plate because the pitcher, who otherwise would be the logical cutoff man, is doing something else. He is backing up the

catcher, in case the throw from the outfield gets past him. In Little League, however, the backstops are so close, the fences and screens so adjacent to home plate, that not only is the pitcher not needed to back up the catcher—frequently there isn't even room for him to be there.

2. Not only the closeness of the backstop, but the small size of the Little League infield itself—remember, it is less than half the square footage of a regulation infield—leaves the pitcher with no place to go. Inevitably, he will serve to clutter up the play.

3. Use of the first baseman as cutoff man in such a situation deprives the defending team of anyone at first base. Suppose the first baseman cuts off the throw and the hitter has overturned first base and now scampers to get back. He is free to do so because first base is uncovered. In the major leagues, he is free to get back to first because there are not enough men to deploy into the cutoff situation and still cover first too. In Little League, however, the logical use of the pitcher as cutoff man leaves the first baseman free to stay on first base, and thus can result in a put-out impossible under regulation circumstances.

To those three reasons we might add a fourth: namely, that, all things being equal, the pitcher in a Little League game is, as often as not, the best player on the team. Thus, from the standpoint not only of the physical mechanics but of individual judgment and ability, he qualifies additionally to be cutoff man.

Some Little League teams have no cutoff play at all. When, in the opinion of the manager, they seem to be sophisticated enough to employ such a play, "sophistication" too often becomes the same as "professional," and therefore automatically the first baseman become the cutoff man. After all, the professionals don't use the pitcher for that purpose. No one stops to realize that the reason they don't is that in their game they can't.

But in Little League it can be done. And should be done.

The point here is not without interest. The observant manager or coach will do more than acknowledge the fact that a Little League diamond is smaller than a regulation diamond. He will even do more than teach his boys within the framework of that limitation. Ideally, he will understand that limitation—and then take advantage of it!

This means that in several important ways the manager and coach will want to think about departures from standard baseball procedure. In so doing, the teacher can be comforted by the fact that he is not "ruining" a boy's baseball future by invoking special techniques that apply to Little League only. Certain things that are taught at the Little League level have got to be untaught in any event, as a boy grows older. All too often overlooked, in the meantime, is the simple postulate that the object of coaching in Little League should be to turn out not good baseball players but good *Little League* baseball players.

The coach who bears this basic distinction in mind is likely to encounter, sooner or later, a further paradox—but this one highly satisfying and rewarding. For the more he teaches his players as Little Leaguers, the more they will begin to look like Big Leaguers!

This book, we hasten to say at this point, is not

intended to be a guarantor of champions, all-stars, or victory at the annual Little League World Series at Williamsport. A coach whose team is blessed from top to bottom with proven individual ability, or a manager who can draw from many teams in putting together an all-star club, may or may not stand to benefit from somebody else's instructional tips. Either way, however, he is rich in playing talent, and that sets him apart immediately as a vivid exception to the hundreds of thousands of managers and coaches throughout the Little League program whose no less devoted task must be to guide their teams through the ups and downs of a normal Little League season, and whose ambition is met by the sight of seeing their boys play better in June than they did in May—and enjoying themselves while they're at it.

To a degree probably far greater than anyone wishes officially to acknowledge, much of this depends on the boys themselves. A great deal has been written about the so-called "abuses" and "overemphasis" of Little League, and commercialization, and parental interference, and all the rest. This book was designed basically to be a coaching manual, and so it will touch only peripherally on such fringe elements. But one point might be made here, which is that while it is generally accepted that effective coaching can help produce victory, far less understood is the corollary principle that victory can help produce effective coaching. Little Leaguers have sensitive ears, and the same instructional pointer that they will gladly accept as constructive criticism after they have won a game has a way of sounding like blame after they have lost.

Philosophically, the author's own position on the

importance of winning might be expressed in paraphrase of the milkman in *Fiddler on the Roof:* namely, that while it's no disgrace to lose, it's no great honor either. Those who feel that every boy should appear equally, or even partially, in every game represent an area of thought which takes into consideration all elements—except, sometimes, the players themselves. It is wrong never to let a nine-year-old into a game. It is equally wrong to send him up to bat against the best pitcher in the league simply for the sake of getting him into the game. Coming up ten times with a chance of reaching base strikes most youngsters as preferable to coming up thirty times and striking out. Avoiding those thirty strikeouts will doubtless help the team. *It will also help the boy!*

Here again is a situation which reflects the *growth* of Little League more than anything basically wrong in the program itself. By process of proliferation, Little League has done more than multiply into the millions the numbers of players. It has also doubled the number of adults. It is a fair rule of thumb that each new player means two additional adults, usually parents, and the manager or coach is faced with the dismal reality that a youngster's problems spin off from his father's or mother's. In truth, this reality is so dismal that many coaches tend to blame their problems en masse on the vicissitudes of home life, up to and including their own coaching mistakes. One of the most perceptive comments, in contrast, that we ever heard from a coach was his sad indictment of one of his youthful players: "He has a nice mother, a nice father, two nice sisters, and one nice brother. He himself is a bum." This happens too.

Perhaps this book can serve the accidental side

purpose of breaking down the differences between so-called "major league" and "minor league" configurations in Little League play. Many people feel that at the "major league" level within Little League, it is all right for a team to field its best men and try to win, but that at the "minor league" or "farm team" level, everybody should get into every game. While we have no quarrel with the idea of distinguishing between the levels of skills, or proportionate older and younger ages, expressed by the "major" and "minor" programs, it is the intent of this book to express not the differences but the similarities in basic coaching technique.

No doubt there are—and will be found in these pages—degrees of complexity and sophistication which, basic physical skills being equal, the older boy will grasp and his younger brother will not. But in essence, they are playing on the same-size diamond under the same rules, and this, as has been pointed out already, exerts a commanding influence overall.

The basic fundamentals are the same, and are taught the same. Not the age nor the relative comprehension of the boys, but the field itself, is what says this must be so. In fact, there exists an interesting statistical proof of this. It is to be found, of all places, not in hitting, not in pitching, not in baserunning, not in umpiring—but in fielding.

In the National League in 1966, the fourth-place team finished first in team fielding; the seventh-place team finished second; the second-place team finished ninth. This was a wholly typical professional result. The correlation between winning and fielding percentage is that there is no correlation at all.

By contrast, in Little League—regardless of what

level of Little League we consider—the team with the best fielding average is almost inevitably the team that wins the most games.

There are four basic reasons why this is true:

1. The dimensions of the field itself. The distortions Little League imposes upon the race between runner and ball are considerable. In the professional Big League, a team may average better than two second-to-first double plays on ground balls for every three games played; in Little League, a team that turns in two such double plays in its entire season is a curiosity.

2. A story is told about Yogi Berra who, in his days as a rookie with the Yankees under manager Bucky Harris, tended to swing at very bad pitches. "*Think* before you swing!" Harris urged him. Berra went up to the plate, struck out, and returned grumpily to the dugout. "How can you think and hit at the same time?" he complained. At Little League age, the biggest problem is to think and *field* at the same time. The great preponderance of errors comes with men on base, when boys are required not only to execute more functions but to plan that execution in the very act of fielding the ball.

3. Faced with the shortage of double plays and the complications of "field-think," one reason Little League pennant winners show good fielding averages is that they are not confronted with too many enemy base runners to begin with. In this respect, good fielding and good pitching go hand in hand. The more opposing batsmen who strike out, the fewer the fielders' opportunities to do something wrong.

4. At Little League age, the good fielders are

usually the good all-around players. Not only can they catch and throw the ball, but they can run and hit too.

All of these factors being present, the startling thing is how much a good coach can do about them. The coach cannot change the size of the field, nor do his fielders' thinking for them in mid-play, nor pull an extra-strong pitcher, hitter, or runner out of his hat.

He can, however, initiate schemes which, like the cutoff play outlined earlier in this chapter, eliminate enemy base runners not in spite of field dimensions but because of them. He can drill his players in an interesting form of "situation practice" which gets them into the habit of doing their thinking before they get the ball, not at the moment they get it or after.

Most important of all, he can work with physical fundamentals—and here, it makes no difference whether he is dealing with "major" or "minor" Little Leaguers. That is one of the reasons this book will deal at particular length with *fielding* fundamentals, for they are equally beneficial to the youngest and oldest, the least and most experienced, boys in the Little League program.

That is, to repeat, one of the reasons. It is not the primary reason. The primary reason is almost mysterious to relate, but it is very real nonetheless. And this is that good basic fielding habits have a way of releasing and promoting a boy's best potential in the other aspects of the game.

Alertness in the field has a way of guaranteeing similar alertness at bat and on the bases. The nine positions come to bat only one at a time, but on defense any one or more of the nine can be called into play at any given moment. That is yet another reason contributing to our belief that defense ought to be worked on first of all.

And there is still another element, which is what one might call the "impatience quotient." It is in fielding, contrasted to the other branches of the game, where mistakes can be corrected the fastest —sometimes in a single stroke. The look on a boy's face when, with one simple change in his *foot*-work, he discovers he can *throw* a ball 30 feet farther than ever in his life before can be something to behold.

What deserves consideration, too, is the fact that boys of Little League age—especially those trying out for the first time—take most naturally to fielding, as opposed to other phases of the game. Very few youngsters, at the time they come into Little League, have ever pitched competitively; a remarkable number have never swung a bat. All of them, however, have "played catch," one way or another, dating back to their days as toddlers or even before. And a good teaching program builds from the familiar rather than the unfamiliar.

Preseason tryouts, preceding the "auction" that will assign new boys to various teams, have the weakness of exposing faults without disclosing how serious—that is, how resistant to correction—any given fault may be in the case of any given boy. Typically, a youngster will get three or four fly balls hit to him, with instructions to throw home. Then he will be given six to ten swings of the bat, with instructions to run to first after the final swing. The assembled managers will thus get a passing look at the boy as he hits, catches, throws, and runs. For all their brevity and imperfection, these tryouts are quite sound. The manager gets to see the very good and the hopelessly bad.

What he does not get to see is the desire that may or may not accompany the very good and the hopelessly bad. It is a little too glib to say that the better a boy plays the game, the more he must want to play it. It would be a lot easier on the coach if this were true. But the fact of the matter is that, not infrequently, the worst player is the most eager of all, while his more skilled friends cut practice, miss games, and sometimes drop out altogether. Even eagerness itself requires some inspection: there are times when it stems more from parental pressure, or even from some inborn conviction that this is the only way to be "one of the crowd," than from any intrinsic enthusiasm.

Here, then, is just one more powerful factor setting Little League baseball apart from the game played by older boys; for at the Little League level many things masquerade as desire. There are places, unhappy to relate, where participation in Little League is regarded as a social necessity. Strictly from the coaching standpoint, the bad thing about that is that sometimes it takes the coach half a season to catch on.

And yet, here again there is something the coach can do about it. By making the game interesting for his players—by getting the *fun* out of fundamentals—he not only subscribes to the Little League ideal that every boy finds a home on one team or another; in so doing, he can well take a giant step toward turning out a winning team. A good basic rule is that enthusiasm, particularly in practice drills, can be contagious.

Some of this enthusiasm will radiate from the

manager and coaches themselves; indeed, if they didn't have it, they would not themselves last long in the program. But there is no more miserable sight than that of a coach who cannot communicate his own enjoyment to his players. The most frequent reason for this, when it happens, is, to put it bluntly, that the coach doesn't know what he's doing.

And there is no automatic reason why he should. The majority of Little League managers and coaches emigrate, at least to begin with, from the ranks of those whose knowledge of the game proves, when put to the test, to be inadequate. There is no reason why this should not be so. At the Little League level, the players are not the only ones who may have no particular interest in baseball as a career. The adults, too, include those who regard Little League not as a chance to develop a specific skill in a specific sport, but instead as the prevailing organized activity for boys of that age at that time of year. And this, perhaps, is the most strange among all the consequences of the growth of Little League.

Putting it another way, the years have developed more baseball-minded boys than baseball-minded men. The market in skills among boys reaching Little League age is by now controlled only by the birthrate. But the market in men to teach them has, as a result of the growth of the program, become understandably short. The demand for more coaches has produced a shortage of available adults who know what baseball is really about (it is no rap against the coaches to observe that most of them *think* they know, because the most casual fan *thinks* he knows).

And yet, as has been said earlier in this chapter, salvation does not lie in turning to professional baseball men for advice, because (as Willie Mays says) the one thing worse than undercoaching at the Little League level is overcoaching.

Examples of this are legion. Take the case of a Little League hitter who can hit fast balls but not curves. He is up against a curve-ball pitcher, who throws two curves in a row and misses with both, so the count is now two balls and no strikes. Now enter the overzealous manager who has "hit" and "take" signs for his batters. With a 2-and-0 count, he sniffs the base on balls and flashes the "take" sign, ordering his batsman not to swing at the next pitch.

On the surface, it looks like the soundest thing to do. It is, in fact, the one worst thing that could possibly happen. No kid pitcher who has missed twice with his curve ball is going to come back with it a third consecutive time. Not only is he going to come in now with the fast ball, but most probably he is even going to "aim" it.

Simply, what has happened therefore is that our "over-coach," with all his "knowledge" and "signs," has literally ordered his hitter not to swing at the best pitch he's going to see!

There we have a case of a manager who "knew" too much baseball. Equally unnerving are the cases of those who don't, but who overcoach anyway. The author was witness, some years ago, to a situation where, with a man on first and two out, a young third baseman came in to charge a ground ball, then, in getting the ball to first, threw it away. His overconscientious manager called time out and went out to talk to the boy. He pointed out that the easier play, because of the shorter throw, was the inning-ending force throw to second.

This manager was wrong on the face of it to call time out during a game in order to bawl out one of his players, regardless of constructive intent. Worse than that, he was giving the kid bad advice. Perhaps in linear feet the throw to second was shorter than the throw to first. But even with the prohibition against taking a lead, the base runner in Little League still has a head start over the hitter. And the bodily momentum of the third baseman, as he came in for the ball, was more toward first than toward second. And given anything resembling a choice, with two out you *always* play for the batter rather than the runner.

Here, then, was a case where bad execution served to mask the fact that the third baseman knew the right play and his manager didn't. This, too, we can classify as "overcoaching"—of a particularly insidious sort, since the experience could cause the boy to try his best to do the wrong thing in the future.

What confronts the manager in Little League, therefore, is the prospect that he can overcoach whether he knows baseball or not. It is to this dilemma also that this book is addressed.

Little League can be a stranger and more wonderful world than many suppose. There is at least one complicated play that boys of Little League age master faster and better than major leaguers. There is another basic maneuver which, for some reason, is automatically taught the wrong way. These things, and many more, we will attempt to cover in these pages.

Readers may observe the absence in this book of

photographs, drawings, diagrams. This was planned deliberately, from our experience of a few too many cases where pictorial supplements hurt more than they helped. Baseball instruction, especially for pre-teen youngsters, is hard to depict pictorially. Perhaps this is because a picture, "frozen" in time, too often shows what may be "right" at the moment the photo was snapped, but proves to be either wrong or meaningless in the full development of the process we are trying to illustrate. This is particularly true, and most commonly found, in photographs of the "ready" positions of great hitters. Each of them may take a slightly different stance, yet, as that pitch rides in, they all cock the bat the same.

A technical (if that's the word for it) note deserves to be underlined here, and that is that the great majority of Little Leaguers both throw and hit right-handed. For that reason, this book will, in discussing hands, arms, feet, and legs, assume that the pupil is right-handed all the way. In the case of a left-handed thrower and/or hitter, obviously the prescribed positions reverse, with "left" becoming "right" and "right" becoming "left."

An effort also will be made, where possible within the framework of this manual, to examine elements that have to do not only with coaching but with outside pressures and the conduct of games generally. This effort will be reflected, typically, in the sections on umpiring and on methods to give the younger or part-time player a chance to perform without necessarily detracting from the chances of the team itself. In these areas too, some surprises await.

As a matter of fact, Little League is a game of

surprises—and in this respect it does not differ at all from baseball as played by older boys or professionals. In the many years of our connection with Little League, we have seen no more rewarding sight than that of an old man who came to watch the Little Leaguers play, day in and day out. He had no grandsons playing on any of the teams. In fact, locally he had no family at all.

He came to watch a ball game.

[2]

Fundamentals in Fielding

Maybe the first thing to be said about basic pre-season practice for Little Leaguers is that such drills ought to depend as little as possible on the availability of the community's Little League playing field. Bad weather, early nightfall, overdemand for use of the field, and the absence of the last-minute repairs and work that will get the field ready for opening day all conspire to give a hit-or-miss aspect to field conditions in late March and early April, so the majority of workouts are likely to take place on grounds other than the exactly tailored diamond which will be the scene of play once the season actually starts.

The frequent existence of such jerry-built circumstances has a way of bothering managers and coaches more than the boys themselves; and indeed it is surprising how much good basic work can be gotten in even in the absence of such seasonal amenities as raised pitcher's mounds, outfield fences, well-rolled infields, or premeasured distances. Some kind of fencing—perhaps no more than an embankment in the ground itself—is of course desirable for hitting practice, but even this is more of a prop to contain foul balls than anything needful to the teaching process itself.

In some ways, actually, too good a field can be a handicap in the initial going, because it can be an invitation, especially to older boys—some coaches, too—to gloss over fundamentals and get down to "game conditions." This is obviously bad for the new players; maybe not so obviously, it can also be bad for the more experienced boys, many of whom have talent that in previous seasons has disguised the possibility that they too may be doing something fundamentally wrong. Scarcely a season will go by in a given Little League, for example, that will fail to produce at least a couple of all-star pitchers who don't know how to pitch, and who not only could be even better than they are but could also reduce considerably the risk of a sore arm or worse if only they'd do it the right way.

The right way, incidentally, is basically exactly the same for non-pitchers as for pitchers, and the fundamentals in throwing a baseball deserve to be first matter of business for a manager preparing his team for the season that lies ahead.

Not only the first, but every ensuing, practice drill should begin with the manager pairing off his players, two by two, to "play catch." As players' arms get used to throwing the ball, these sessions can begin to be longer, both in point of time and as to the distance between the players. A good rule at the beginning might be ten to fifteen minutes with a throwing distance of 35–50 feet between players. This can be gradually lengthened to fifteen to twenty minutes and 45–60 feet as time goes by.

At the first drill, major attention should be paid to the use of the feet while throwing. Basically, there are two ways of doing it wrong. Either the boy steps forward with the wrong foot, with the result that he "throws like a girl," or he does not step at all. It is surprising how many youngsters will exhibit one of these two defects.

The right way is to step forward with the "throwing foot"—*i.e.*, the foot opposite the arm that does the throwing: the left foot for a right-handed thrower, the right foot for a left-handed thrower. This foot should make contact with the ground *before* the ball is released, but not so much before that the arm has not yet gone into its throwing motion. Ideally, the throwing arm will be cocked and will be coming forward on a plane with the thrower's neck and ear (depending on whether he throws most naturally tending toward the sidearm or toward the overhand), but will not yet have released the ball, at the time the throwing foot comes down.

This is simpler even than it sounds, yet for many youngsters it comes as a revelation. It is easy to spot them when they are doing it wrong, and it comes naturally for them to correct the delivery once it has been pointed out to them. At that point, typically, the boy who has been doing it wrong will now throw the next one ten feet over his intended receiver's head. He never knew he had such strength!

The manager can confine himself, in the initial drill, to correcting this fundamental fault—and to seeing to it that none of his players is trying to cut loose and abuse his arm by throwing too hard.

In subsequent practice sessions, attention can be paid to "scatter-arms." One simple device can be employed to accomplish two distinctly different things—and here again, this one simple device dramatizes the close connection between throwing and pitching.

Let the player take a position like that of a pitcher, with his feet comfortably planted, 9 to 12 inches apart, and the toe of the throwing foot even with the heel of the other foot. Then let him bring his shoulders slightly forward and rock his arms, just as a pitcher will do, one to three times before the two hands come together at his chest and he proceeds with his throw. This "rocking chair" motion is a near-perfect guarantee of a controlled throw, because it fixes not just the arm, but the body itself, on the target.

But it is more than just a guarantor of accuracy. Any manager or coach can prove this to himself at home, through a simple exercise. First, he should stand erect and pretend he is throwing a ball without moving his feet. Next, go through a throwing motion while stepping forward with the throwing foot, as described above. Finally, try the rocking motion and follow through with the whole body.

"Throwing" a ball without moving the feet, you will feel the effect of the throw in the upper forearm, just below the elbow. When you step and throw, you will feel it in the upper arm, between elbow and shoulder. When you rock before you step and throw, you will now feel it in your shoulder and back.

In this graphic manner, a coach can convince himself of the soundness behind the medical argu-

ment that most sore arms in Little League youngsters can be traced to "too much arm" and not
enough body in the way some boys throw. The
"rocking chair" motion, therefore, serves not only
to produce more accurate throws but also to curb
the risk of injury.

Of course, we do not expect catchers, infielders
or outfielders to throw with a "rocking chair"
motion during a game. By the same token, they do
not do that much of any kind of hard throwing
during a game. Once learned at the beginning of
practice, however, the motion has the residual effect of putting a boy's body into the way he
throws, which in turn helps his throws to be on
target, and so it is of basic value to non-pitchers
and pitchers alike.

The same game of catch which will reveal any
underlying flaw in the way a boy throws a ball
will, of course, also display any faults in the way he
catches it. This is a somewhat more complicated
area, not only because fielding a ball involves more
facets of the game than getting rid of it, but also
because of an element of fear.

At Little League age, this is wholly understand-
able. Indeed, before trying out for Little League, a
surprising number of youngsters have never had
anything to do with a hardball in their lives; and
whereas they can readily adapt to new and better
ways to cast the ball away from themselves, the
ball coming at them is something else again.

It is all very well to chant "Two hands for
beginners!" but the coach who does so ought to
know *why* two hands are better for beginners.

It does not make too much sense to tell a boy he
will catch the ball better with two hands when he

33

obviously catches it better with just one. And most newcomers to Little League do their best catching with gloved hand only. To many of them, the glove is their shield; to quite a few, it is, in fact, a matador's cape, held over to one side, so that if by any chance the ball misses connections with the glove, it won't connect with the human being attached to the glove.

Here once again is a case not limited just to newcomers. Boys who have been in Little League for two and three years can be seen still trying to catch a ball off to one side—and therein lies the *real* reason why two hands are better. Getting a youngster into the fundamental habit of using two hands when a ball comes his way has the effect of lining him up with the oncoming ball. This creates an element of balance in the fielder, and the balanced fielder not only performs better, but is far less open to injury, than his unbalanced compatriot.

Simply explaining this to a young player is not going to convince him. Instead, there are two steps that usually prove effective in the case of a boy who persists in catching the ball off to one side. First, show him that you want both hands in front of him as he gets ready to take the throw (not too hard a throw, please). Second, ask him to see how fast he can get rid of the ball once he catches it! This is a stunt, and it has to be done one boy at a time (otherwise the team-wide game of catch will turn into a giggling shambles). But it's a challenge that appeals to the youngster, and subtly converts him to two hands instead of one, because, being against the clock, he will find it difficult to get rid of the ball in a hurry unless the hand that does the throwing is adjacent to the glove when the catch is made.

When instructing the neophyte to hold his hands in front of him when expecting a throw, don't lock his hands into a frozen position, or they may never unlock. It is surprising how many Little Leaguers try to "vest-pocket" a catch of a ball thrown at their necks, and even how many more try to slap *down* on low throws. (Once in a while it's standard to field a grounder at a fairly low level with the palm down, but that is because no slapping motion is involved—the momentum of the ball is sending it up into the glove; the player is not coming down on it.)

A good way to start things out, therefore, is to have the waiting player place his hands before him, at about stomach height, palms facing, as though they were holding the sides of an invisible ten-inch box. (This is a good state of readiness for the hands not only for thrown balls, but in advance of batted balls as well.)

Many boys instinctively shift their hands to handle different kinds of arriving throws. For those who have trouble, there is a simple, pleasant, and rewarding kind of exercise. Let the boy stand with his hands over his head, palms facing away from him, thumbs together. Now let him gradually lower his hands. As they reach chest level they begin to turn inward so that at stomach level the palms are facing each other, and at belt level they have begun to unfold the other way, till finally they arrive at their lowest point—thigh level— palms once again facing away from the boy but with not the thumbs, but the pinkies, side by side. Let the boy do this several times, then go through the same routine but starting at the bottom and going up.

The delightful discovery to be made from this simple exercise is that if you stop the hands at any point in mid-motion, from top to bottom or bottom to top, they will automatically be in the ideal position to catch a thrown ball at that particular level. Another nice thing is that it is impossible to do wrong.

If the throw is so far to either side that the player cannot get his body in front of it, the technique is even simpler. For such throws to the glove-hand side, the player simply sticks his glove hand out, thumb up, and whether high, middle, or low, that is how he will catch the ball. Conversely, if the throw is to the bare-hand side, the player crosses the glove hand in front of his body, thumb down, and the same thing occurs. A *low* throw to the non-glove side, however, can also sometimes be handled by twisting the wrist. There is no set formula for this one type of catch.

A word here about the manufacture and wearing of baseball gloves today. Time was when the first baseman was the only fielder whose glove was designed to be worn "off the hand." Today, all fielders' mitts are larger and longer, and in professional ball few if any players remain who still center the palm in the glove. The advantages are longer reach and less wear and tear on the hand from a "direct hit" (though a player soon learns to "give" with a ball as it strikes his glove, to cushion the impact). The disadvantage is that sometimes it is hard to get the ball out of the glove once you've caught it.

An additional disadvantage to Little Leaguers is that their hands are boy-sized, not man-sized, and controlling today's gloves can become a problem therefore. Too many fathers think they are doing their sons a favor by equipping them with major-league-model gloves. It is, in fact, the worst thing they can do at that stage in a boy's career, and it is no solution to say the boy should put his fingers all the way into the glove anyway, because the glove will still be far too big. The best thing a manager can do is to encourage the use of smaller gloves—the big companies do make Little League models, and there is nothing "sissy" about using them.

If a boy does have a large fielder's glove, he will control it best by putting the hand in the glove as far as possible while still leaving the index finger *outside* the glove, behind the backstrap. If the excess padding in a new glove becomes a problem, a solution is to apply oil to the front surface of the glove, then fold it like a claw and place it nighttimes under a big dictionary or some other form of weight. This at least will make it more malleable.

As we have noted, there are several different areas to be discussed when it comes to catching a ball. Catching a throw is different from fielding a grounder; fielding a grounder is different from catching a fly; and especially considering the number of balls in Little League that don't quite "get there," the scoop, or short-hop pickup, of a thrown or batted ball becomes an added science in itself.

Here once again, however, the major attention of the teacher should be focused first not on the hands but the feet. We have discussed correct fielding position for the thrown ball. Correct fielding position for the batted ball comes next, and this is the same for all seven non-battery positions.

As a pitch is delivered, every boy in the field

should be in the position of a racehorse jockey: semi-crouched, weight on toes, heels up. There is a comfortable point that can be reached here; also an exaggerated point. We do not want to go to the exaggerated point, where if the pitch is a slow ball instead of a fast one the fielder will fall over on his face. But stopping short of that, this is to defensive baseball what the Arthur Murray "magic step" was to dancing. Here are some of the things it does:

1. It enables the boy to break in any direction— not only forward, but, using either or both sets of toes as a "push-off," to either side or back.

2. It provides a fair guarantee that the boy will play the ball, rather than vice versa. Not only errors, but injuries, are a common consequence when the boy backs up as a grounder comes toward him. The boy who is up on his toes to begin with is not nearly so likely to do this as the boy who is planted on his heels.

3. *It is an automatic guarantee of mental attitude!* Mental concentration has a physical base— all of us have experienced, for example, how much easier it is to listen to a conversation when our *eyes* are on the speaker, and how difficult it is to listen and look elsewhere at the same time. So it is with this basic fielding position in Little League baseball. The boy who is taking the right physical position as the pitch is delivered is automatically in physical focus with the game he is playing. Thus his concentration is assured: built-in, so to speak.

At the professional level, all infielders take this stance just before every pitch. Outfielders don't, mainly because they are far removed from the hitter and don't have to involve themselves in charging the bunt or the topped grounder. But they are still paying attention.

Because the attention span is so much shorter in Little League, and because the outfielders are stationed considerably closer to the bat, we suggest that they at least be drilled to take the infielder's stance before each pitch, as an aid to concentration and as an antidote to standing flat-footed.

In fact, it isn't a bad idea to treat everyone on the team as an infielder during the first practice sessions. The game of catch can be followed by a session in which the manager and/or coach hits— or, even better at this stage, throws—grounders to the boys.

In this way, two things can begin to be taught: first, the correct preliminary stance; second, the way to field a ground ball once it is hit. For the latter purpose, the manager should restrict the grounders in this drill to the kind the boy can come in on. They do not have to be aimed directly at the fielder in every instance, but they should be the kind to permit an incoming motion in the act of fielding. Since perhaps 75 percent or even more of the ground balls hit to the infielders during a regular game permit this incoming action on the fielder's part, there is nothing wrong with restricting the grounders to that variety during these early drills.

As a boy comes in for a ground ball, the step he takes as he actually fields the ball should be with his *throwing* foot (*i.e.*, a right-hander's *left* foot) whenever possible. On ground balls hit to the extreme right of a right-handed fielder, or left of a left-hander, this sometimes cannot be done—but bear in mind that for now we are discussing only the common garden variety of grounder, on which the player's main motion, even though at an angle, is forward.

The manager need not worry unduly about a boy's ability to "hit" with the proper foot. Once it is explained to him, the execution itself will draw on a natural instinct—the same instinct a hurdler or a running broad-jumper always calls on to take off from a preferred foot.

The next question is: Why "hit" with the *throwing* foot while fielding a grounder? The answer here may best be displayed if we break down the process of fielding a ground ball into consecutive steps:

1. Player breaks in toward oncoming ball.
2. Player's left (throwing) foot comes down and he fields ball.
3. As he straightens for the throw, his right foot, in automatic momentum, now comes down.
4. Now the left foot, once again, as he makes his throw.

Suddenly, as we examine this numbered breakdown, something interesting jumps into focus: fielding a ground ball is only half the battle! Unless you're within short running distance of an unassisted put-out, you still have to throw it too. And you throw with your "throwing" foot—as in Step 4 above. To make Step 4 possible, nine times out of ten there must be the intervening Step 3 to account for what happens with the feet as the body, already in motion, straightens for the throw.

What we have created with this step-by-step process, therefore, is the continuous flowing motion of fielding and throwing together. Sometimes, as when a grounder is a sharp one-bouncer or takes a very high hop, Step 3 can be eliminated; other times, as when the boy has to range far to either side, or back, it is meaningless if not impossible. But on the vast majority of ground balls, this is the sequence that will be called into play, and once having mastered it, the boy will automatically adjust to the minority of "off" plays.

In teaching this sequence, the manager will if nothing else have accomplished the singular achievement of treating ground balls for what they are—the start of a play, not the finish. Too many sources of baseball advice treat the fielding of ground balls as an end in itself. To repeat, it is clearly not the end—it's the very opposite: the beginning.

But this sequence will do other things too. Once again, it will tend to bring the hands together, because coming down on the left foot tends to bring the ungloved right hand in toward the glove. Here, therefore, is one more subliminal encouragement to field with two hands instead of one, which in turn gets the body in front of the ball!

This, in its own turn, produces balance. Balance, in its own turn, helps the boy play the ball instead of the ball's playing him. The more he plays the ball, instead of vice versa, the less chance he has of being hurt, even by a bad hop. One of the reasons he will not be hurt is that he is selecting which bounce of the ball he will time himself to take. And this, in its own final turn, has got to mean cleaner fielding and more put-outs.

In all of this, we assume that the ball, when fielded, will be as close as possible to midway between the player's legs—this is just restating the necessity mentioned above to get the body in front of the ball. Of the three categories of ground-ball errors that can be corrected by proper coaching, perhaps the most common is the off-balance situation where the ball actually strikes one of the fielder's feet, or strikes the glove and is immediately dislodged as the glove strikes the foot. Some boys will need more practice on this than others, but it can be corrected. Get a well-balanced body in front of the ball, and it won't happen.

The second most common mistake on grounders is the so-called failure to "get the apron down." The ball goes right through the boy's legs. His glove comes up and the ball doesn't. This is almost always the result of a fielder's stationary posture—here again, the ball is playing him. The boy moving in on a grounder can preselect the moment of contact. For the boy who stands and waits, the ball will do the selecting.

The third type of correctible error was referred to in passing a little bit ago. Some boys love to slap down on grounders as though swatting a bug. As noted earlier, there is a way to deal with this.

We have not mentioned at any point here how far the feet should be spread apart while fielding grounders because if the two basic points—correct preliminary stance and correct footwork—are properly accounted for, this element will largely take care of itself. Obviously, an extreme stance—feet together or hopelessly spread apart—should be modified, but whatever spread between those extremes proves most comfortable for the player is the stance he should take.

In discussing the kinds of errors that can be made on ground balls, we held off mention of two other mistakes common not only to grounders but to the fielding of fly balls as well. One of these is a tendency to close the glove before the ball gets there; the other is the attempt to throw the ball before it is actually caught. These don't happen very often, and when they do they reflect an over-anxiety on the part of the fielder, which in turn produces a kind of error that *does* happen with some frequency.

What happens here is that, having failed to come up cleanly with the ball, the boy now panics and kicks it, plays patty-cake with it, or throws it away. Sometimes a chain reaction sets in, with three and even four fielders handling the ball on the same play and all of them doing it wrong.

Sometimes, these sad processes reverse themselves: having dropped a ball, a boy now wants nothing to do with it; or, having fielded it apathetically, he finally throws it and discovers the whole team is asleep.

The most common single demonstration of this comes when a boy, having lost his grip on the ball because of a fall or a collision, simply lies there, with no attempt at recovery.

Anyone who has watched as few as a dozen major-league games knows that these extremes of panic and apathy can set in, for no accountable reason, with professionals as well as amateurs. They are mental in origin, albeit physical in result, and so there is no concrete practice drill—outside of continuing exposure to the game of baseball—that can help.

One difference between the pros and the Little Leaguers in this type of instance lies not in the player but in the manager. If the manager or coach tends to be volatile or apathetic at the Little League level, his players are much more likely to reflect his temperament in the way they perform.

Because the apathy factor is as real in its own way as the panic factor at the other end of the spectrum, the coach who never criticizes is as bad in his way as the coach who yells all the time. It should be borne in mind, however, that the fielder who falls asleep does so before the ball is hit to him. If a ball gets past a boy because he wasn't paying attention, the manager should have seen this before the play, not after. If the ball goes past him because he's out of position, that's the manager's fault 100 percent. The one unforgivable zone of criticism, as mentioned in the previous chapter, is criticism stemming from the manager's own ignorance.

Furthermore, actual "turning points" in baseball are far fewer than the sports pages would want us to believe. If a fielding error in the last inning permits the only run of the game, is that therefore the turning point? What about back in the second inning, when you had bases loaded with one out and didn't score?

In 809 games played in the National League in 1966, a total of 6,624 runs was scored—an average of better than 8 runs a game. This if anything should stand as proof positive that baseball games were not designed to be settled by 1–0 scores. We have seen a Big League game settled by a 3-run homer, which came about by C's hitting the home run after A had walked, stolen second, and B had then been issued an intentional base on balls. The "turning point" in the next day's papers was the home run. Actually, though, A should have been out stealing; the catcher made a delayed throw. Once on second, and following the intentional pass to B, A was in a position to pick off the catcher's sign and relay it to C, who now hit his home run because he knew what the pitch would be. Multiply this by the fact that they score 8 runs a game in the majors, and it is not only the wise, but the truthful, coach who, having lost a game, will find reasons aplenty over and above the one pitching or fielding lapse that accounted for the winning run.

As a general rule, a boy ought not to be condemned for a physical error. (Even this has its exceptions—sometimes, when the game didn't depend on it even remotely, it is a good thing to dress down one of your better and more cocksure players. It's good for him and the rest of the team both.)

Most basic, with respect to the subject of fielding, is this: if a boy has made an initial error, calm but articulate temperament and instruction from his manager can help keep him from compounding it with a panic play. Indeed, many times the initial error can still produce the intended put-out.

"Stay with the ball—but don't lose your cool." This, in shorthand, is the best instruction a manager can give. But he must live by that word not only in preseason practice but throughout the Little League year, and not only by word but by his own attitude.

Meanwhile, the basic lessons in stance and motion will have gone a long way to prevent basic blunders. If the basic stance is essential to picking up a ground ball, it is equally so for catching a fly.

Infield flies, because they have less trajectory, are actually more difficult to catch than outfield flies. Even a good outfielder can behave like a clown under a fly ball in the infield. In fact, the most universal—almost instinctive—misplay in Little League is the case of the boy who plants himself under an infield fly, and then, having planted himself, cannot unplant. Inevitably, the ball will come down five to ten feet *behind* the point where he has stationed himself. And, being planted now on his heels, he is in no shape to back up.

This can be corrected. It is corrected by repeated practicing of one skill. Once mastered, it governs the boy's fly-catching ability not only as an infielder but as an outfielder as well. It also has the side virtue that it avoids the boy's injuring himself by collision with a fence or another fielder.

It is the one most basic fly-catching technique, *and yet it is practically never taught!*

"Keep your eye on the ball"—this is basic baseball teaching.

And it causes nothing but trouble.

"Take your eye *off* the ball"—that is the real secret!

If that statement has an arresting effect, this was the purpose behind it. Of course we do not expect a boy to catch a fly ball without having his eye on it. But most if not all of them can learn not to be hypnotized by the ball so that they stumble and fail to untrack. To be able to look away from the ball in its mid-flight, long enough to gauge the distance to a fence or another player, or long enough to turn one's back and retreat forward instead of backward, is a key to catching balls safely which otherwise would have fallen for base hits. It's also a way to decrease the risk of injury through collision either with inanimate or animate objects. A boy who can learn to look away, even for a fraction of a second, has mastered a truly basic fundamental in defending against the ball hit in the air.

The remedy consists of throwing fly balls to the boys, gradually increasing the height of each fly. We suggest throwing to them rather than hitting with a fungo bat because the thrown ball is far easier for most coaches to control. (The notion that a batted ball behaves differently from a thrown ball is, in a mild way, correct, but that means a ball hit *against a pitch*—thrown balls and fungo-hit balls behave alike.)

This is a drill that can take place beginning with the earliest practice session, and its duration is limited by how much the manager's arm can stand. It's good to have a coach help out. Even a couple of your better twelve-year-olds can share the throwing duties—but watch their arms as well as your own.

As soon as a player has demonstrated that he can catch a fly, he is ready to progress to the next step: throw him a fly, let him pick up the flight of the ball, then order him to look at some preselected ground-level object for a brief period (don't worry how brief—the boys themselves will make it quick) before he looks back at the ball and makes the catch.

Once he can do this, the next step is to throw him flies that will land 10 to 20 feet behind where he is standing, and have him pick up the flight of the ball, then turn his back and circle to catch the ball as it comes down.

This isn't a one-shot exercise, and it isn't necessarily for the whole team, either. Some boys obviously won't need this kind of practice, and others are going to require more work on fundamentals before it will do them much good. But employ due care before you excuse a youngster from this particular drill. Some boys will pick this up much faster than other, even more fundamental, skills. A surprising number of others can do all things well except this. At the post-season all-star level of Little League play, involving only the older and most talented players, perhaps the most common misplay comes on those "Texas League" flies, too close in for the outfielder to get, where the infielder, backpedaling slowly and clumsily or refusing to take his eye off the ball (which would enable him to turn his back and run full out), fails to make the catch.

And the reason he doesn't make the catch is that nobody ever taught him the play. Talent and instinct alone don't guarantee that it will occur to him, unless there's somebody to point it out to begin with.

We recall one practice session, between games during a season, when the manager was drilling the entire team—except one boy, his own son, who played second base. The coach had him off to one side, throwing those "Texas Leaguers" at him, one after another. The boy could handle every part of playing second base except that one. It took something like sixty throws before the coach was satisfied (either satisfied or exhausted, perhaps a combination of the two).

The very next game was ended, with a winning result, when the boy turned his back, dug out into right-center field, turned, and caught a "Texas Leaguer" for the final out. The look on his face was equaled only by the look on the face of the long-suffering coach. One of the joys of properly conducted practice sessions is the discovery, not only by the players but also by the men who teach them, that practice does pay off!

Basic drills for outfielders per se will be discussed in an ensuing chapter. It is not recommended that these be a part of team-wide practices during the early going, because they are boring, do not by themselves do any real teaching, and are seldom applicable to league play, where the outfield positions, particularly left and right, are often the "learning" spots for younger boys.

At any given point during batting practice, however, boys waiting for their turn to hit can rotate at another part of the field into a fly-catching drill conducted by a coach who will either throw or fungo-hit a succession of fly balls to the ever-changing cast of receivers.

In such instances, it is a great temptation for the coach to combine running with fielding and make the boys go a long way, left to right, to gather in the ball. This is the way they do it in the major leagues. It is a false invitation to copy it. An adult player can "run off" a weight problem, but if a youngster has that kind of problem, running by itself won't help him. And the easiest fly ball to catch is the one where the young player can "draw a bead" or "get the angle" to his right or left. In such drills, rather than run him sideways, run him in and out. The great running one-handed catch, where the boy goes a magnificent distance to his left or to his right, is in reality the simplest of plays—assuming he doesn't crack a fence or another player en route. That is why learning to take the eye off the ball produces not only better fielding but better safety, and it applies as much to the infielder challenging a foul as to an outfielder challenging a fence—or to two fielders challenging each other. The ability to check the location of some obstacle while in full pursuit of the baseball not only locates the object but assists the pursuit.

In any event, learning to gauge the ball that will drop before or behind him is far tougher for the outfielder than gathering in the ball to either side.

The epitome in this respect is the line drive hit directly at the outfielder. Will it dip and fall in front of him or will it soar and go over his head?

The solution, for the manager and the coach, must be a thankfulness that such situations arise as seldom as they do. When hit in that fashion, a fast pitch will tend to stay up; a slow pitch will tend to fall. But even that isn't a rule across the board. There is just no way to teach it.

Handling the pickup or scoop—the throw that bounces just in front of the fielder—is something that can be helped by prolonged practice sessions. Many coaches deplore the tendency of a boy to turn his head away while attempting to field such a ball. Actually, this is human nature—for the ball that isn't cleanly scooped is likely to ricochet, sometimes up against the player's body, and nobody wants it to hit him in the face. Also, turning the head at the last minute doesn't affect the boy's chances of making the pickup. By that time, the head and eyes have nothing to do with it.

The closer the glove is to the ball when it strikes the ground, the better the chance the pickup will be made cleanly. It is not an easy play, and even the good fielder will mess it up with some degree of regularity. Generally speaking, though, the most common mistake made on this play occurs when the fielder tries to make the pickup on a ball that hits the dirt too far in front of his glove. The glove is held at ground level on pickup plays, but when the ball has room to bounce, it will hop over the glove. A good way to work on this is to throw the boy not only balls that bounce immediately in front of him, but once in a while one that bounces five or six feet in front of him. He will then begin to sense when not to stretch forward for the attempted pickup, but instead to pull back and field the ball on its normal bounce.

That would be one of the singularly few instances where we would advise a player not to go out and meet the ball. Whether it is the body charging a grounder, the hands being held at head height or even higher in catching a fly, or the glove out in front of the body to take a throw, the basic overall key to good fielding is to go out to meet the ball—as opposed to having the ball come in to meet you.

[3]

Fundamentals in Batting

Unlike fielding, the basic fundamentals in batting cannot be taught group-style; nor do boys readily correct their own mistakes for seeing them in others. Some players will obviously need more work than others, but they must be worked with individually.

It should go without saying at the outset (yet some coaches overlook it) that the smaller the physical size of the boy, the lighter the bat he should use. (Perhaps strangely, the converse does not necessarily hold true—a big boy may be more comfortable swinging a lighter bat; this ought not to be encouraged, but it ought not to be forbidden either.)

Also unlike fielding, certain players will have advanced far enough, or have displayed the natural ability to begin with, so that they simply do not need any real work in batting fundamentals. For some hitters, the only trouble a boy experiences will come to light during the season, not before—

usually on account of some effective way of pitching to him discovered by the other teams. (Although it may be inappropriate in this chapter, this is nevertheless a logical place to suggest to managers the value of watching other teams' games during the season. Not only batting weaknesses but any number of other habits—a catcher who delays his throw, a third baseman who plays too wide of his bag, a pitcher who cannot field bunts, a base runner who wanders too far off first after the pitch has crossed home plate—can in this fashion be spotted and taken into account for your own next game against that team. Bases are stolen, runners are advanced, other runners are picked off, more on account of what the opposition did wrong than what you do right.)

Having suggested that the small boys swing the light bats, we hasten to add that physical size ought never to be confused with maturity or skill. A very small twelve-year-old may have the wrists, the forearms, and the eyesight to swing a big bat. This, however, is a rank exception to the rule.

We mention the lower arms, the wrists, and the vision, because—perhaps sad to relate—these alone produce a truly good hitter. In the absence of all three, no amount of teaching will advance the boy beyond a certain predestined plateau as a hitter. In the presence of all three, very little teaching is needed; if the boy does have weaknesses, a word from you might help, but he will also be tending to correct them himself.

The idea that shoulders and body and legs go into what makes up a good hitter is a myth. Even home-run range, Little League fences being as close in as they are, is not controlled by size or heft.

Given a set of eyes that can "pick up" a pitch and the power of strong forearms and the snap of good wrists, the smallest boy on the team can hit the ball out of the park. And lacking all these requisites, the biggest boy can't, save for some dazzling once-in-a-lifetime accident.

We must not expect, therefore, that a low-grade hitter will hit high-grade pitching. But the low-grade hitter can be taught to hit low-grade pitching, and the confidence that comes with this may enable him to hit medium-grade pitching as well. Similarly, the medium-grade hitter can be taught to hit medium-grade pitching, and he in turn will then get an occasional hit off high-grade pitching.

Just as in the fundamentals of fielding, the basic problem to newcomers in hitting is fear itself—even more pronounced in batting than in fielding. As mentioned earlier in this book, every eight- or nine-year-old has played catch at one time or another, but a surprising number have never even held a bat before.

The more a boy plays and the older he gets, this fear will of course recede, and yet if it is not dealt with at the outset, the bad form dictated by fear today will remain the bad habit of tomorrow, even though by then the youngster is no longer afraid.

The classic example here is that of the player who closes his eyes when he swings. At first this is a reflex act of flinching. Let it go uncorrected, and four years later he will still be closing his eyes.

The most basic principle in batting is a negative one: you can't hit what you can't see. The way to deal with this, some coaches believe, is to start their younger players off with easy (sometimes even underhand) pitching from short distance. We disagree with this approach. The pitches should be easy, yes, but they should be delivered in normal style from normal distance. The feeling here is that *everything* that is taught in practice, no matter how rudimentary, should bear the strongest resemblance possible to the requirements of the game itself. To proceed by simple steps—simple both in themselves and in their stages of progression—is one thing; but deliberately to make any one step an artificial distortion of the game is something else, and not to be encouraged.

It is not artificial, however, to make sure that a boy wears a batting helmet—or, at least, one of those protective sets of "ears"—even during easy practice pitching. This is not only a rule during games, but a sound practice—and a comfort as well—during batting drills.

The two elements that most conspire to keep bat from making contact with ball are, in order, a boy's closing his eyes or turning his head; and a boy's stepping back as the ball approaches. The reactions in both cases are basically fear-induced.

Yet neither can be dealt with properly till two other elements—a good grip and a good stance—have been accomplished. Good grip and good stance create confidence, and confidence helps outlaw the other bad signs induced by fear.

Thus, before a youngster ever even sees a practice pitch, there are some things to be done.

Grip comes first—all other things can be worked on later, but the basic question of how to hold a bat has to be dealt with at the outset. Among other things, it brings to light those occasional curios who like to bat one-handed or cross-handed, and that, in turn, points up the perplexing fact that there are many different ways to hit a ball. Be that as it may, there remains only one way to hold a bat.

On the basis of putting first things first, it isn't a bad idea to determine whether the boy is a right-handed or a left-handed batsman. Ninety-six times out of a hundred, he will instinctively do the choosing for you and automatically bat the way he feels most comfortable. And at the Little League level, ninety times out of a hundred he will bat the way he throws—right-handed, if he's a right-handed thrower, left-handed if he is a left-handed thrower.

By the time a player reaches the rarefied atmosphere of the professional major leagues, there will be a greater proportion of hitters who throw one way and bat the other, but the specialties of the chosen few are seldom visible in boys of Little League age.

If, once a boy has been subjected to all the different basic suggestions for batting fundamentals, he still seems awkward for no apparent reason, it is worth finding out not only how he throws but how he writes, how he plays Ping-Pong, and so on, in search of some indication of at least partial ambidexterity that is worth the experiment of switching him around at the plate. In fact, once in a very great while, an authentic switch-hitter appears at the age of nine, and there would probably be more of them if managers and coaches ever bothered to wonder about it.

The overwhelming majority, however, will instinctively choose the favored hitting direction, either right or left. And as they do so, taking a few practice cuts with the bat, the manager can judge from the way they swing whether the bat is too heavy or too light.

To do this, he should approach the right-handed batsman and make sure that his left hand is snugged down at the bottom of the bat so that the bat is held *tightly*. The manager then takes the player's right hand, places it fairly high on the bat, and then in an abrupt motion forces the right hand down till it is firmly against the left hand and gripping the bat just as tightly.

This is the way to hold a bat.

Now have him take some practice swings. If the bat is swinging him, it is too heavy. If he is whipping the bat, it is too light. If the lightest bat seems still too heavy, then and only then should you consider having him "choke up," holding the bat somewhat higher up than down at the handle.

It is true that some players who can swing a bat properly while holding it down at the handle prefer to "choke up" anyway—and may even hit better that way.

If they do, it can be discovered by experimentation later on. The point being made here is that, while not opposed to "choking up"—indeed, we actually favor it in many instances, particularly in the case of younger boys—we are definitely opposed to doing it automatically at the very beginning. Too many managers and coaches make this mistake without ever thinking of one curious and basic fact of Little League baseball.

That fact is that although the boys are shorter, the bats are shorter, and the dimensions are shorter in Little League as opposed to regulation size, *home plate is the same!* It is 17 inches across in Big League, and it is 17 inches across in Little League.

That gives the Little Leaguer, with his shorter arms and shorter bat, the task of protecting a strike zone equal in size to that of a major leaguer. The only concession Little League makes is to place the batter's box 4 inches away from home plate, as opposed to the regulation 6. But this pick-up of 2 inches is more than canceled by the length of the bat alone, with the common Little League range of 28–32 inches countered in the regulation game by an average of at least 5 inches longer. Add to that disadvantage the shorter length of a youngster's arms, and the ability to pull the outside pitch, or at least hit it to center field, involves itself in a tremendous physical disparity.

One method of overcoming this is to teach youngsters from the outset to take a position as close to the plate as possible while still remaining within the batter's box. This not only gives them added reach, but provides two psychological advantages as well:

1. A young pitcher, facing a batsman who crowds the plate, is reluctant to try for the inside strike for fear of hitting the batter.

2. When the batter is crowding the plate, Little League umpires tend to call the inside-corner strike a ball—because the pitch comes so close to the hitter. By contrast, let the batter stand well back in the batter's box and the umpire tends to call a strike on the pitch which is 1, 2, even 3 inches inside the plate.

Above all, however, the wise manager or coach will not give in to the temptation to order a small newcomer to "choke up" automatically. First see if he can swing the bat down at the handle.

And, by teaching him the grip outlined in the preceding paragraphs, the coach will also have seen to it that the two mistakes in gripping the bat—the only two that can be made, really: hands holding the bat too loosely, hands not together—will not be present.

(Is it possible, incidentally, to grip the bat *too* tightly? Most of the experts say yes. We don't believe so. What is possible is for the boy's whole body to be so rigid that he needs to be told to let up, to gentle, to relax, but a too-tight hold on the bat, while it may accompany an overall sin, is no sin per se.)

Stance comes after grip, and here things are by no means so simple. There may be only one way to hold a bat but, as previously noted, there are any number of ways to hit a ball. Many elements go into a good batting stance, but let all other things be equal, the boy who is "book-perfect" in each individual element might hit the ball better if he weren't.

The reason for this is that good hitting stance—and when we say stance, we include stride and follow-through—is composed of so many different parts that good hitting habits depend as much on the way the youngster puts the parts together as it does on whether he knows each one separately.

So there are few absolute rules. One of these is that a fidgety hitter seldom connects. Once the pitcher is into his windup, the batsman's head *must never move*. Neither should the feet, although there will be an almost instinctive shifting of the weight slightly more onto the back foot as the pitch comes in. Similarly, the only movement of the arms will be a slight "cocking" motion which, again, comes as a reflex to good hitters. It is almost physically impossible, even for a bad hitter, to swing at a ball—if his grip and stance are otherwise correct—without moving the arms slightly backward as the pitch nears the plate.

This rearward cocking motion becomes more pronounced, of course, when the hitter's eyes have signaled his arms that the approaching pitch is going to be measurably slower than expected. There is really no other way to consume the extra time it takes the slow pitch to arrive.

(This tends to explain, by the way, why the one pitch that consistently fools the good hitters in Little League is the unexpected change-up. They are so gifted at not moving when the pitch is en route that the extra degree of back hitch is something that comes hard to them—and so, willy-nilly, they swing early.)

A second firm rule is that a hitter who drops his back elbow in the act of swinging will automatically be hacking up on the ball.

If, as he waits for the pitch, a player's wrists are about even with his rear foot, and held at about chest height, if his rear forearm is on a plane about at a right angle to his body, then he is "book-perfect" in the way his arms are being used as the pitch approaches. But he will spoil the whole thing if, in the act of swinging, his rear elbow is allowed to drop. (Note that you cannot drop your back elbow while swinging without at the same time artificially twisting your wrists—which in turn means that all the power of wrist snap, which is the secret of good hitting, is lost to you.)

Therefore, as the player swings, there should be no sudden drop of the back elbow the instant the swing commences. The elbow instead should travel, as much as possible, along a horizontal plane. (We say "as much as possible." Many things, including the player's build and the location of the pitch—high or low—keep this from being an inflexible teaching.)

The manager in doubt as to how to spot this should watch the player's wrists as much as the rear elbow. If they twist, and the bat travels in an upward arc, correct the "elbow drop" and the swing will correct itself.

The front elbow has importance too, with respect to a level swing. Held too low, it causes the player to hit down on the ball. Some coaches have believed that instead it should be held high—so high that the rear elbow is forced to drop. In this case, the hitter actually uses his front elbow as a gunsight. It is a persuasive notion, except for the fact that the higher the front elbow is held, the less the batter will be able to connect with the low inside pitch. The low inside pitch and the high outside pitch are the easiest to hit. In our opinion, the player ought not to be hampered in his ability to hit either one of them, for there is everything to be gained, and nothing to be lost, in teaching a youngster from the very beginning along lines that will enable him not only to get the bat on the ball, but to connect solidly when he does. A boy's satisfaction from hitting a ball well, as opposed merely to making contact, is obviously enhanced many times, and helps produce confidence.

If the back elbow is held correctly, and the grip on the bat is right, the front elbow will almost automatically do what it is supposed to do for that particular player, so by concentrating on back elbow and grip, the manager or coach will usually not have to worry about the front elbow at all. Note that if the front elbow is held too high, the bottom hand on the bat will tend to "peel off"; if too low, the upper hand on the bat may do the same. Thus if the grip is right to begin with, it is likely that the problem will never come up.

Another nonexistent "problem" is the angle of the bat itself to the player's body. If grip and stance are basically correct, this will take care of itself, because the end result—the best possible swing—will have to be the same regardless of the position of the bat before the swing commences. As a rule of thumb, the closer the boy's stance, the more the bat will tend to angle toward the horizontal; the wider apart his feet, the more he will tend to hold the bat vertically, or even actually slanting slightly inward toward his body.

The timing of the player's swing has as much to do with *stride* as anything else. A player who strides early, late, or—in a few flat-footed inept cases—not at all, is losing whatever power he has. The forward foot should, in proper stride, make contact with the ground an infinitesimal fraction of a second before the bat makes contact with the ball.

No such specific advice, however, can be given as to the *length* of the stride. This will depend on the location of the pitch, the build of the hitter, and how closely together he holds his feet in his basic batting stance—which last-named factor is, in turn, largely a matter of what makes the player feel most comfortable.

While good eyesight, wrists, and forearms are the requisites for the great hitter, obviously grip, balance, and feet must play their parts too—for without these in proper function, the great hitter will be only a good hitter, the good hitter a mediocre hitter, the mediocre hitter no hitter at all.

The comfort and build of the boy himself will,

as we have noted above, mainly dictate how far apart his feet will be held in his basic batting stance. Perhaps a front-to-back spread of 12 inches is a useful rule, but this can vary. A boy who consistently overstrides should widen his stance; a boy with too short a stride should hold his feet closer together.

What is vital, however, is the basic distribution of weight and the way the feet are "planted." The rear foot definitely is "planted," firmly dug in and placed flat against the ground. It should never move until the body in mid-swing pulls it up and around into the classic "tiptoe" of the rear foot in the follow-through.

The front foot, by contrast, is in "soft" contact with the ground, and may even be held with the heel raised. The more it is raised, the more the hitter's weight will shift onto the back foot. This is not totally a bad idea against fast-ball pitching.

In any event, in the swing and follow-through, the front and rear feet will trade roles, so to speak. The planted back foot will, as noted above, wind up on tiptoe; the unplanted front foot will wind up planted at the end of its stride.

Part of the flexibility in batting style is the degree of crouch in any given hitter's stance. Ordinarily, the farther the legs are held apart, the less crouch there will be, but that's about as much as this text would want to say on that subject. (The observation can be made, however, that a tall boy with an erect batting stance is giving away an extra-big strike zone. Even then, if that's the way he hits best, that's the way he should stand.)

It is a matter almost of individual taste whether the player's front foot is closer to the plate than his back foot, or the other way around, or both feet equidistant. In stepping into a pitch (assuming here a pitch over the center of the plate) a hitter should tend to compensate automatically. If his front foot is closer to the plate than his rear foot, the front foot will tend to step away from the plate, for example.

In Little League, however, there are two good reasons why the front foot ought to be closer to the plate.

The first of these reasons goes back to the curious artificiality mentioned earlier, in which home plate in Little League is just as wide as in regulation baseball. It is a way to get the player closer to the plate so he can cover it fully with his bat, yet still leave him full power for the inside pitch.

The second reason lies in the tendency of Little Leaguers to "step in the bucket," pulling away from the pitch. If the boy starts with his front foot already distant from the plate, he can wind up halfway back to the dugout.

The back foot also can give way, as we also mentioned earlier—again, the product of early fear. If you can get the boy to plant his back foot and not move it, this will be no problem. But if, despite instructions, the tendency to back off remains strong, there is an ingenious stunt that works as a corrective, and sometimes as a full cure. Have the player take his proper stance in batting practice. Then take a bat and place it on the ground, in a straight line parallel to the long lines of the batter's box, directly behind his back foot.

The object of the "game" is of course for the hitter to take his swings, pitch after pitch, without ever disturbing the bat on the ground behind him. We have seen it work time and again.

Even if you do everything right, some boys "reflex" slower than others, and late swingers will come around late with the bat. Constant practice, the use of a light bat, even "choking up," will help this—as much as it can be helped. One other device will help it too. Have such a boy take the heaviest bat on the team, and have him swing it constantly—even letting him take it home at night with him. Then, when he actually comes up to hit in practice or in a game, switch him over to the lightest bat.

This advice is probably good for every hitter on the team. Actually, it is such a standard procedure that professional hitters waiting their turn at bat inevitably and automatically swing two and even three bats—the object being the same, namely, to make the bat seem lighter when they actually get up to swing. But the special application of this advantage to the chronic late swinger ought not to go overlooked.

The problem of the chronic early hitter is seldom found in Little League. With the pitcher's mound only 46 feet away, few are the bats that come around before the pitch gets there—excepting only the case of overslow pitching, or, as previously noted, the occasional unexpected change-up.

In fact, it is opposition pitching, rather than any set rules for your own hitters, that will dictate whether your hitters stand forward in the batter's box or farther back. Against fast pitching, hitters should stand farther back in the box—giving themselves the greatest distance from the pitcher's mound, thus the most time to bring the bat around. Against slow pitching or curves, it is better to stand forward in the box. Against pitchers who have both a fast ball and a curve, it is better to stand back in the box to guard against the fast ball and take a chance on the curve.

Most Little League curve balls bend rather than break. By standing back in the box against a pitcher who also has a fast ball, a boy can guard against the fast one and at least break even against the curve. The curve that winds up outside may be tough for him to hit, but the curve that ends up bending over the plate becomes easy. (It was Casey Stengel who made the deathless observation that "a curve ball over the plate ain't a curve.")

Strangely, curve-ball pitching does not seem to accentuate what is already the worst single fault any Little League hitter can have: the inclination to swing at bad pitches. No matter what kind of pitch is thrown, boys will try to hit the bad ones— and there is no known cure for it, outside of constant verbal entreaty: "Make it be good. . . . Don't help him. . . . Wait for your pitch. . . . A walk's as good as a hit," and so forth. This constant patter from the dugout will at least serve to remind the hitter that there is such a thing known as a strike zone. It does no good to say you can't get a hit off a bad pitch, because you can.

The opposite of the player who chases the bad ones is the one, usually the frightened newcomer, who doesn't swing at all. Here would be one case where you might urge a boy to bunt rather than swing away, as a means of giving him confidence and helping him keep his eye on the ball (by facing the pitcher).

We do not hold with some coaches who have an automatic rule that this is all a young player should be permitted to do when at bat during, say, his en-

66

tire first season as a Little Leaguer. Spotted against the proper pitching, he should get the feel of swinging away too, and the earlier the better.

But we definitely do recommend bunting as a basic part of hitting fundamentals, not to be practiced later but to be worked into batting drills from the very outset. The bunt not only has the advantages listed above, but is an integral weapon in any Little League offense—not so much as a means to move a man from first to second, but as a strong element of attack in many other situations. The fielding of bunts comes hard to Little League youngsters, and any defender who must run, pick up the ball, and throw it is called upon not only to make decisions but to execute several different moves. The chance to force the error is therefore highest of all in this situation.

It can be said bluntly and truthfully that the bunt is the one thing in all Little League baseball that is most often taught the wrong way. Not the part about holding the bat: that is standard. The upper hand on the bat is slid about halfway up the bat and held by the fingers, thumb on top, so that they do not protrude to the "hitting edge" and thus risk a boy's getting hit in the hand by the pitch. The bunting itself is then done with the fat upper half of the bat beyond the fingers.

The wrong part is the way youngsters are most commonly taught to swing to face the pitcher as they take the bunting position. Most managers teach the boys to pivot on the rear foot, thereby swinging the front foot away and back from its original position.

This leaves the boy in what amounts to the rearmost corner of the batter's box, and from that position he finds it almost impossible to bunt fair, if he can make contact at all, if the pitch is over the outside half of the plate.

We have asked many managers why they insist on teaching this, and their answer has always been that to pivot on the front foot will wind up with the boy's "stepping on the plate"—that is, he will have to step out of the batter's box as he brings his rear foot forward.

This would be true if the front foot were used as a pivot. But it need not so be used. The correct thing, instead, is to have the boy step away from the plate with his front foot as he turns to face the pitcher, at the same time bringing his rear foot forward to occupy the space where the front foot has been.

This rapid two-step leaves the boy in perfect position to bunt anything in the strike zone—and he is still very much within the batter's box.

The act of bunting in the squared-away posture is by itself, we think, also mistaught in many instances. Some teach that the hitter should push the bat at the ball. Others say the bat should be "drawn back" and the ball allowed to, in effect, "bounce" off it. Still others believe the bottom hand should be used to steady the bat while the upper hand guides the bat into the ball.

In actuality, we believe neither hand should predominate. Both hands should be raised, for example, to bunt the higher pitch, both hands lowered for the lower pitch, so that the hands are always on a level with each other and the bat, therefore, in a horizontal position.

As for pushing the bat into the ball, or drawing away from it, here again perhaps the best way is to do neither. An almost imperceptible "nudge" of the bat into the ball as it arrives produces the best bunt, because it combines control of where the ball will go with control of not bunting the ball too hard so that it goes directly and at once back to the pitcher.

This kind of bunting, where the hitter swings his body to face the pitcher as the ball is delivered, is, we believe, the only kind that should be taught as a part of basic hitting fundamentals. The push bunt and the drag bunt, executed as a surprise at the last second, have their places, especially for left-handed hitters who are a solid couple of steps closer to first base to begin with, but the squared-away posture is the only one that ought to be taught at the beginning—and frequently the only one a team will really need and use all season long.

If any one basic essential for hitting should be stressed above all else, it would have to be the need to keep the eye on the ball—and its essential is *never* to move the head, from the time the pitcher winds up till either the ball is past the plate or the swing has been completed. Once in a while even a good hitter will turn his head at the moment bat meets ball . . . and get only a piece of it as a result. Holding the head steady and watching the ball at all times not only make for confidence and better hitting, but insure safety as well, since the steady and conscientious eye will pick up the errant pitch earlier and signal the body to get out of its way.

Patience and constant practice are requisites too. Artificial aids, like hitting tees or pitching machines, don't do any noticeable harm, but at the Little League level they are subject to the abuse of being treated as substitutes for human effort, and as such they don't do any good either.

[4]

Fundamentals in Running

In a sense, the very title of this chapter is misleading, for baserunning involves far more than fundamentals, and much of it cannot be taught as part of any basic drills at the very beginning. Knowing how to slide is important (mainly for the slider's own bodily safety). Knowing *when* to slide is far more important, and there is no way to teach this at the start or all at once.

Indeed, if it comes down to a choice between the two, a manager would have to prefer a smart runner over a fast runner.

The smart runner knows how many are out, what the score is, what inning it is, the relative speed (and brains too) of another runner on base ahead of him, the throwing and general fielding capacities of his individual opponents, the comparative strength or weakness of his own teammates next due up at bat.

Sheer speed, without any thought behind it, has

an embarrassing way of getting a boy safely to a base already occupied by another teammate. The non-thinker tags up when he should be going half-way or all out, and vice versa. He slides at the wrong time and at the wrong base, and then lies there, under some kind of illusion—surprisingly commonplace—that because he is stretched on the ground, the play must be over.

This is not to make fun of boys who don't think, because there is very little correlation, if any, be-tween I.Q. and the ability to "instinct" what is, in truth, a game of almost endless possibilities and subtleties.

The best thing a Little League manager can do is put a team in the field, have a group of other boys act as "runners," call out various situations, then hit the ball at random choice to one fielder or another. (Note: Fielders and runners can be more or less rotated so everyone gets a chance to do all things, and the runner who acts as the batter should start late to duplicate actual game conditions in which the hitter is always a step or two, in point of time, late in getting under way as he recoils from hitting the ball.)

Even this, however, is not a fundamental drill. You cannot assign a boy to play shortstop till you know if he can pick up the ball, and even then you may have no intention of using him as a short-stop. And, as considerations like those might sug-gest, these "situations," while of tremendous value, do a lot more for fielders than for base runners.

After each situation play unfolds, however, the good manager will speak not only to his fielders but also to his runners. Though it is primarily a defensive exercise, the boy who is not going all out

71

when two are out is running badly, and his failure to run is just as correctible as the failure of an infielder getting a two-out grounder and trying to get him at home instead of throwing to first.

Another thing "situations" can teach runners is to round a base instead of simply pulling up to a stop. The safe feeling Little Leaguers get when they reach the next base often keeps them from the extra steps and momentum that either legitimately on the hit itself, or on account of a defensive mistake, would gain them an extra base.

Nothing so characterizes Little League games as the kind of "shadowgraph" stop-and-go effect where, with ball in play and runners in motion, everything stops for a long instant, then just as suddenly picks up and continues.

The aggressive teams are the ones whose runners are always moving forward, always alert to the possibility of the extra base. Nor do we confuse this with the sins of oversliding or overrunning a base. Things like that can and often do result in outs. But alert, aware advance beyond a base is something quite different, and if once in a while it produces an out, the net gain is still overwhelming.

One tactic can be mentioned here by way of example. It is seldom used, unless the situation is so blatant that it provides its own invitation. It should be used a lot more.

Suppose you have a good runner on third base, a weak hitter at bat, and two out. At any point where the catcher drops the ball, or it rolls a little away from him, the catcher will tend to do the following: he will go to where the ball is, look at the runner leading off third, then throw it back to the pitcher. That is the key, right there, and just as runners should be alerted to take advantage of it, catchers should be taught not to let it happen.

The correct thing is for the catcher to bring the ball back to the plate with him, then throw it back to the pitcher. If he throws it from where he picked it up, and the runner from third suddenly breaks for home, the runner has at least a fair chance of scoring even on a short passed ball, because the catcher must not only take the return throw from the pitcher but get back to home plate, all at one and the same time, thus reducing the chances for a clean tag.

(We say "even on a short passed ball." We might almost say "*only* on a short passed ball," because the farther the ball rolls away from the plate, the more likely it is that the pitcher will come in to cover home as the catcher retrieves the ball. It is on those plays where the pitcher doesn't see the need of covering the plate that the runner from third can explode for home, the instant the out-of-position catcher throws back to the mound.)

This situation arises with remarkable frequency, and given the fact of two out and a weak hitter at bat, the offensive team has little to lose. Get that weak hitter behind in the count—at no balls and two strikes, or 1-and-2, even 2-and-2—and instead of having little to lose you have absolutely nothing to lose.

For some strange reason, you can work this play time and again, even against the same opponents, and they will never correct the basic defensive mistake that makes it possible. Perhaps it is the preoccupation of the moment that leads them to forget next time around.

(By curious contrast, a good catcher-to-first

pick-off play usually works only once. The word grapevines around the league, and enemy runners don't take idly excessive leads off first base from that moment on. Which is all right too. If you can keep a base runner honest without having to throw the ball, you're that much ahead.)

Instructions in the fundamentals of baserunning must also take into consideration, once again, the physical differences between Little League and professional baseball. In the pro leagues, for example, it is mandatory for the man on third (unless he represents a totally meaningless run) to come home—regardless of his chances of making it—when, in a first-and-third situation with nobody out, the batter hits a double-play grounder. In Little League, as noted previously, there is practically no such thing as a double-play grounder. Thus the purpose of the man on third to head for the plate in order to preclude the double play is not the purpose of a Little League man on third. The play in the majors is to save the extra out. In Little League, there is no fear of the extra out.

And so it is difficult, at any level, to separate baserunning as a physical science from the situation in which it occurs.

Certain points can be made:

1. Boys should understand that in overrunning first base, the only likelihood of their being put out is if they make an overt move toward second. It's fashionable to suppose that the hitter is safe only if he overruns first in foul territory, but it doesn't happen to be true. He can overrun in fair territory too, without jeopardy, so long as he does not commit toward the next base.

2. A most common baserunning mistake in

Little League (to compensate, it is least often properly appealed, or noticed by umpires to begin with) is simply to miss a base while in transit. Whole scientific tracts have been issued proving it is better to hit the base with the inside—or outside —foot while going on to the next base. Our belief is that it is better to hit the base, period, and never mind which foot.

3. Taking things one at a time, the conscientious manager will talk to his runners about their actions when two are out, before discussing the one- or none-out situations. Under such circumstances, they *must run on anything.* And they must run *all out!* The boy who "loafs" home from second on a base hit with two out, on the quite proper assumption that there is no way the defense can throw him out at home, may find himself arriving at the plate after the outfielder has thrown to second to get the hitter trying to stretch his hit from a single to a double. In such a non-force situation, the out at second, being the third out of the inning and being made before the runner from second reaches home, means that the run does not count.

4. In going for an extra base or taking an aggressive turn, the hitter or runner should "run the circle." The closest distance between any two bases is a straight line, but on any opportunity to get more than one base, whether for runner or for hitter, the boy should use the base as a point on an arc, not the point of a square.

5. Like fielders, runners need to keep their eyes on the ball. This does not apply to single-purpose situations such as beating out a ground ball, or coming home when a throw to the plate is expected.

In other situations, however, Little League runners, under actual game conditions, really can benefit from what in regulation baseball is a bad habit, which is to watch the ball as they run.

This is admittedly bad advice anywhere but in Little League. In Little League, however, the thoughtful manager or coach will sooner or later have to come to grips with the reality that his first- and third-base coaches are not nearly so useful as those roles become at the higher levels of the game.

The two functions most often allocated to first- and third-base Big League coaches simply do not exist in Little League—where coaches cannot guide players in taking leads, or warn them back in case of a sudden pick-off throw by the pitcher, because in Little League leads do not exist until the pitch has reached the plate. And if there are signals to be given, they generally come (with one occasional exception—the signal to the man on first to steal second) not from the base coach but from the bench.

The fact emerges therefore that in Little League the base coaches have comparatively little to do. In practice, also, managers usually like to give base-coaching assignments to younger boys who do not get to play very much. In sum, and despite occasional good efforts to do something about it, the maturity, judgment, alertness, and even the interest of a young player do not realistically tend to develop in the role of base coach. So when it comes to a question of somebody's having to help the runner, it may be best if this somebody turns out to be the runner himself.

This does not mean the runner is completely on

his own, or must run bases while constantly looking behind him or over his shoulder. (For one thing, Little League dugouts are usually so close to the playing field that shouted instructions from the bench frequently carry as well as those from the coaching lines.) And there are still those plays —when he bunts or is racing to first base on a grounder; when he is stealing, or advancing on somebody else's grounder; when he is coming home against a thrown ball—when he will just put his head down and run.

But if, on some other plays, the runner occasionally takes a peek at a play developing behind his line of vision, there's quite possibly a net gain at the Little League level. And any habits that form can readily be untaught if he continues in baseball past Little League age.

6. A boy's stance as a base runner differs considerably in Little League from the regulation game. In the regulation game, a runner leads off a base facing the pitcher. In Little League, where the lead can not be taken until the pitch reaches the batter, the boy's stance as the pitcher delivers the ball should be one in which he faces the next base. Using his right foot as an anchor on the base, he is in a "standing start" position, with his left foot a short (*not* a long) stride in the direction of the next base.

As the pitch reaches the plate, he now takes one fast step with his right foot, another with his left, then once more with the right, this time coming down on the right foot so his head does face the infield. If the catcher does not hold on to the ball, the runner now may push off with his right foot and continue toward the next base. If he is stealing,

77

of course he will continue onward, but in case the batter hits a line drive or fly ball that would cause him to have to return to his base in a hurry, or in case the pitch is not swung at and there is nothing to do but return, the right foot, described as the third and final step in the sequence just outlined, now acts equally as a push-off to enable him to get back.

This combines maximum lead off base with best potential of either continuing onward or returning.

7. While not discounting sliding as a factor in baserunning, we think it is overdone in Little League today.

But before more is said on this subject, one thing must be stressed above all else. Once a boy has decided in his mind to slide, and has committed his body even imperceptibly to it, *he must go through with the slide.* More broken ankles and legs result from a boy's changing his mind in mid-slide than from all other causes put together.

Not infrequently, weather and field conditions during preseason practice sessions and games make it a bad idea to do any sliding whatever. (We have often witnessed preseason games in which, by pre-agreement, the rule was no sliding at all.)

We have seen, also, many cases where a boy who slid was out at home plate whereas he would have been safe had he come in standing up. This is especially likely to happen when the throw to the plate is coming from behind the runner. If he is standing up, the on-target throw has a good chance of hitting him. But if he has gone into a slide, the ball can go through to the catcher instead.

It also must be realized that a boy gets to a base faster by running all out than by sliding at the end.

Why, then, any sliding at all?

A curious but not inaccurate way of putting it would be to say that the chief purpose of a slide is not to avoid a tag but to make sure the boy stays on the base once he gets there. A proper slide brings you to a stop on the base, and that removes the problem of overrunning.

First base can not be overrun (that is to say, the player who does overrun first is not in jeopardy of being put out). What many managers tend to overlook is the fact that home plate cannot be overrun either! This is one of the reasons we suggest fewer slides at the plate. This specific jeopardy, it should be remembered, exists only at second and third bases.

To the extent that sliding is used to avoid a tag, here again exists a factor that frequently goes overlooked. The avoidance of a tag through sliding is far more "up-and-down" than it is "side-to-side." That is to say, the time it takes for the fielder to bring the ball down to the foot of the sliding runner is more significant than whether the slide is off to one side or another. This is an important point, because it minimizes the value of "fancy" slides—hooks, fall-aways, come-ups, head-firsts.

There is a good deal of sophistication in sliding. (There are times, for example, when the hitter should slide into *first* base!) But these sophistications are by and large beyond the capabilities of Little League players, and we therefore think their teaching should be discouraged.

Most youngsters can execute the standard slide,

which consists of coming down on one buttock, with that leg bent, while the opposite foot extends to touch the base. Most youngsters will definitely favor one side or the other. As much as possible, they should aim the extended toe for the side or corner of the base that will give the baseman the farthest and most difficult tag. However, if the baseman is literally holding the ball and waiting for the runner to arrive, then "avoidance," in this sense, becomes impossible, and in such cases it is better for the runner to slide straight into the base, his best hope now being to force the contact that will dislodge the ball from the fielder's grasp.

Sliding practice, if and when you hold it, should in any event, we feel, be limited to this one basic kind of slide. There are two side benefits of such practice. One is that it helps a runner gauge his distance so that he does not commit what is called in professional baseball "the 89-foot slide"—the slide, that is, in which the runner's body comes to a stop one foot (or even more) short of the base. The other side benefit is to have boys work on, and become conscious of, the need to regain their feet as soon as possible afterward. All too frequently, the runner who slides and then just lies there is missing the opportunity to take an extra base.

Alertness on the manager's part, as well as the player's, is a strong contributing factor to good baserunning. So much of a runner's education comes under game conditions that it is up to the manager on the sidelines constantly to remind his runners of the situation at hand: "Run on a ground ball. . . . Two out, run on anything. . . . Don't take any chances," and so on. Such admonitions are helpful to the runner not only under the momentary circumstances, but as part of his continuing familiarization with the nuances of the game.

One warning the manager should never forget to issue is a reminder to his runners any time the next base is occupied. This goes a long way toward preventing one of the most common—and most dismaying—situations in Little League, where a runner advances to a base only to find a teammate already there.

Fundamentals in Pitching

———————

One of the questions most pondered by Little League managers and coaches is which quality ought to be sought first, above all others, in a pitcher. Is it speed? Is it control? Is it stamina?

There is no magic answer. Speed is not good without at least a measure of control. Control by itself is not enough. And even the pitcher who has both is of little help to a team's pitching plans over-all if he can work effectively only over short spans of time.

For all these reasons—and for a vitally important extra reason—it is our belief that at the "major league" level of Little League, managers ought not to try to make pitchers out of boys who are under-size or underweight for their age.

The average- or larger-size boy who, as he tries out for the position of pitcher, displays control but not speed should have the ability built into his body to throw harder than he does. But we cannot ex-pect the same from the smaller boy.

This may not always be true, for there have been many small men who made it big as pitchers in the professional major leagues. (Even there, the true fast ball is the property of the bigger men.) But these are fully matured adults whose bones have finished growing. At Little League age, growth is still in process—and here lies the extra reason for discouraging pitching by smaller boys. It is a medical reason. For their size, they will be asking their arms and bodies to do too much.

We say "arms and bodies" because, as we have observed earlier in these pages, the player who uses his body as well as his arm when he throws will have to be getting a lot more on the ball. This is good for all players. For pitchers it is more than good: it is essential. The "rocking chair" motion recommended for practice sessions should be, in fact, a standard pitching motion. It not only firms up a pitcher's control and puts more behind the ball, but, again medically speaking, it is the surest guarantee against "Little League elbow," an inflammatory condition that most doctors now trace not so much to throwing curves or "trick" pitches as, far more simply, to too much arm and not enough body.

It is popular to say that in the big leagues there is more to pitching than meets the eye. In Little League, there is probably less. There are really very few mysteries attached to it, and most of the apparent complications are man-made, so to speak.

Even the Little League rule book has contributed to an extra atmosphere of mysticism by reprinting the regulation balk rule (all thirteen sections of it) even though this rule exists only to keep pitchers from taking extra advantage of runners leading off base—and leading off base is prohibited by Little

League rules to begin with. The only reason we have been able to discover for the presence of the balk rule in the Little League book is to "keep the boys from falling into bad pitching habits," an excuse which, while not without merit, might seem overzealous in the case of youngsters already subjected to far greater artificialities than this one.

In contemplating his pitching prospects, the Little League manager will also bear in mind that no one will have to be taught to pitch from the stretch position; that most "off" pitches—such as slip pitch, fork ball, palm ball, knuckler—require a hand larger than a Little Leaguer's to deliver in the first place; that the shorter pitching distance is itself a discouragement to "off" pitches—particularly the slider, which for that reason cannot even be said to exist at the Little League level; and that the best control in Little League is exhibited by those pitchers who can throw in the general area of the individual batter's known weakness, as opposed to those pitchers (and there are some) who can "thread the needle" and get the called strike on the corners of the plate.

That last point reflects the fact—and it is a fact—that nothing short of a rare and happy accident can produce umpiring at the Little League level which is skilled at calling balls and strikes.

Practically all Little Leagues, on account of this umpire factor, are what can be called "high strike leagues," for in addition to operating pretty much on blind guesswork where the corners are concerned, plate umpires in Little League have the invariable tendency to call the pitch at the level where it reaches the catcher, not where it crosses the plate; which means in turn that in the case of a pitch tending downward at the end (which means most pitches in Little League) the high ball is called a strike and the low strike is called a ball.

The best thing to do about this is nothing at all. A pitcher who deals in terms of the umpire's skills instead of his own is going to end up "aiming the ball," and the pitcher who aims beforehand—this is true not just of Little League but throughout all baseball—is, for the sake of concentrating on accuracy, taking too much off his pitches.

Also, despite the umpires' tendency to call the high strike, a pitcher who throws high gains nothing. He must throw in terms of the distance between pitcher and batter. The umpire is making his calls in terms of the distance between pitcher and catcher. The answer therefore lies not so much in whether the pitch comes in low or high as in how much altitude it loses between home plate and the catcher's mitt.

It must be remembered too that when a pitcher tires, a sure sign is his tendency to be "wild high." The best catcher's target, therefore, is the low target.

In fact, if there is anything to be done about helping the pitcher withstand the attritions from bad umpiring, it is best done not by the pitcher at all but by the catcher. And in lining up his pitchers for the season to come, the thoughtful manager will select his catchers first.

The better athlete a boy is, the better catcher he will be. Also, with few exceptions, the better pitcher he will be. The team with two good pitchers and one good catcher is particularly blessed. First, it will have three good players. Second, it will remove the need for a pitcher to do the catching when it isn't his turn to pitch. A catcher's exposure to the possibility of an injured throwing hand, while not overgreat if he knows his job, is still the greatest of any position on the team, and it seems a waste to lose a good pitcher because of a catching injury. The manager who takes extra time to develop a good-throwing, seasoned boy into a full-time catcher—if the rest of his roster permits of it—is indulging in no luxury. In any event, good catching has got to be the key not only to a successful season but to successful pitching (and the two add up to pretty much the same thing).

Two basic things a good catcher will do can serve to nullify the bad effects on the pitcher that are brought about by indifferent umpiring.

1. The good catcher will be as close as possible to the hitter. This not only minimizes the umpire-sensitive distance between hitter and catcher. It also helps the pitcher by giving him less real distance to throw the ball. And—though it is tough to convince a boy unless he feels it instinctively—it lessens the chance of injury to the catcher. The principle is really quite the same as that of low-level bombing in warfare: the closer to the target the aircraft flies, the harder it is to hit. The spray effect of the foul tip or the ball in the dirt grows more menacing the farther the catcher is from the hitter. This is a matter of physics, and also of the fact that the farther back a catcher is, the more reflex "reaching" he will do, thus exposing more portions of his body not guarded by his standard protective equipment. Finally, the catcher who squats deep instead of close up, will, this time through unfortunate instinct, tend to have his bare

hand open and the fingertips thus exposed. Close up, he can learn to make a fist till the ball has reached his glove, and this is the greatest finger saver of all.

2. The good catcher will "bring in" every close pitch. That is, his glove will be in motion so that it will, in the act of catching the ball, bring his glove into the strike zone. This is an admitted bit of fakery, and there is no use overdoing it or trying it on the obviously wild ones. But on the close ones, he brings the outside pitch in; he brings the inside pitch out; the high one down; the low one up. And the worse the umpire is—that is, the more he depends not on where the pitch is as it passes the batter but on where it reaches the catcher— the more he will be taken in by this corrective device. Given the combination of a top-grade catcher and a medium-grade pitcher, the catcher will actually get more called strikes than the pitcher!

There are many other prime arguments for strong catching, but the two listed above are placed here because they most of all have a direct effect on the success of the pitcher . . . particularly in terms of the grade of umpiring found in Little League.

Another element which helps eliminate the sensitive "dip" zone between batter and catcher is, of course, hard pitching itself. This is one of three reasons why the fast ball is the best—in the case of many winning pitchers, even the only—pitch to throw. The harder the ball is thrown, the less dip it will have, if any, at the end of its journey.

Another persuasive reason in favor of the fast

ball is that most Little Leaguers can't hit it. The first rule of pitching in Little League is that—given a boy who can throw hard—you *never* "let up" to a bad hitter. If you can throw the ball past him, why give him a slower pitch he can come around on? (This will change as pitchers—and hitters—go on to higher baseball levels. Boys who cannot hit fast pitching in Little League can persevere and learn to hit it; and boys who overswing on the "change" can learn to hold back. At higher levels, pitching begins more and more to depend on the fact that the pitcher knows what's coming and the batter doesn't. But at the Little League level, it hurts your pitcher not at all to have a poor hitter know he is going to see a fast ball. He's not going to hit it anyway.)

The case of good hitters at the Little League level is something else again. This is the group, as indicated heretofore, most likely to be fooled by an unexpected change-up. So this in turn becomes the third basic reason in favor of fast pitching. The change-up, assuming your pitcher can hit the strike zone with it, has great value—if the pitcher also has a fast ball. The slow pitcher's fast ball is the fast pitcher's change-up. Without the threat of the faster pitch, the slower pitch has no effect at all.

Given a fast ball to begin with, therefore, the pitcher can go to work in practice sessions in perfecting a "change" to go with it. But regardless of whether he is a fast-ball pitcher to begin with, there is one other pitch that can be used in Little League: the curve.

We are indebted to many specialists and baseball men, particularly Dr. Eugene Solovieff of San Francisco and Giants pitching coach Larry Jansen,

for articulating the consensus that curve-ball pitching does not necessarily hurt a Little Leaguer's arm
—if he has the size to begin with, if he does not
throw the curve every time, and if he throws with
his body and not just the arm. If any one of those
three conditions is lacking, he should forget about
trying a curve at that age. If all three are present,
he can throw the curve, and with good effect, and
without physically injurious results.

Many young pitchers who experiment with a
curve ball tend to throw it sidearm. Despite a good
rocking motion, rhythmic kick, and smooth
follow-through, the end result here will be too
much dependence on arm and not enough on body,
and for that reason we argue against any sidearm
pitching in Little League.

The properly thrown curve is instead a matter of
grip and wrist snap. Not only for the sake of
physical well-being, but also to mask it as a possible
fast ball, it should be delivered from the same
motion as the fast ball—either overhand or (far
more common, and easier when it comes to throwing a curve) "three-quarter-arm."

As an exercise for himself, the manager can learn
the effect of wrist snap by placing his throwing
arm down alongside his body, palm in toward the
body, and suddenly twisting the wrist so the palm
now faces forward. This is what a pitcher does in
releasing the curve ball.

At the same time, the manager also should experiment by holding the arm in the same position
and suddenly twisting the wrist so that this time
instead of turning outward, the thumb turns back
and the palm winds up facing away from the body.
Up the arm, you will suddenly feel a brand-new

set of tendons brought into play, almost angrily so. What you have just executed is the release motion of the "opposite curve," more commonly known as the screwball. *No Little Leaguer should even experiment with this pitch, let alone try to use it in a game.*

In tentative summary, a boy with a fast ball can get away with that pitch alone. Given the fast ball, he can also make good use of the change-up or letup. Given either, he can also try the curve, so long as he meets the physical requirements listed just previously.

The *grip* for these three pitches is as follows:

Fast Ball: Ball held either across the seams or along seams where seams are closest together. First two fingers on top of ball at time of release. Thumb underneath. No wrist snap.

Curve Ball: Same two fingers on top, usually along seams. Thumb underneath, but slightly "turned in" at knuckle. Sharp snap of wrist at moment of delivery so pitch is "turned over" and actually slides off index finger en route to plate.

Change-up: Same delivery motion as fast ball and curve. Ball held as much with palm as with fingers. Thumb underneath, but tend more to have three, instead of two, fingers on top. "Floating" motion imparted to ball by pulling hand sharply back (without wrist twist) at time of release. Actual speed of change-up depends mainly on speed of normal fast ball. Delivered to a good hitter who is set for a fast ball, the change will be far more effective if its speed is cut by 15 per cent than, say, 40 per cent below normal fast-ball speed. Taking something off the pitch, in other words, is preferable to taking everything off, for if the difference between fast ball and slow ball is too pronounced, the hitter will be given time to reset for the far slower delivery. His stride and swing will be far more upset by the not-quite-so-fast delivery than by one of total contrast.

Generally speaking, unless his reputation from previous games or previous times at bat for the same hitter in this game has done the setting up for him, the pitcher should set up the change by throwing the fast ball first. A pitcher who has both a fast ball and a curve should rely on the fast ball and use the curve and letup pitch interchangeably. A pitcher who has a slow ball and a curve should use the curve as his main pitch to good hitters, and the change to throw them off stride. The pitcher who has only a slow ball or only a curve should not be pitching, if not for his team's health then for his own.

What has been stated above is a general rule. If a pitcher has both a fast ball and a curve, and not much of a change-up, he will of course want to concentrate on the curve to the good fast-ball hitter. Pronounced individual weaknesses in any given batter should always be exploited, even to the exclusion of any other pitch, if the pitcher can take advantage of it. If you have a pitcher who can throw curves and a hitter who can hit anything but a curve, you throw him curves.

Once the pitcher has started out with the fast ball, the off pitch or the breaking pitch become additional weapons, on account of contrast, in his favor. The hitter will now incline to be guessing, and that has got to be in the pitcher's favor.

But we do not want the catcher to be guessing too. Ordinarily, we advise against any catcher's signals in Little League, unless they are meaningless dummy signs to throw the opposition off. A catcher set for the fast ball can handle the slower change-up without any previous notice. If, however, he has a pitcher who has both a good fast ball and a good curve, he should know which to expect. In those cases, the manager should decide in advance whose judgment he trusts the most—the pitcher's or the catcher's. If it is the pitcher's, then let the catcher signal for the fast ball and have the pitcher shake him off; the catcher now knows the curve is coming. If it is the catcher's, then let the catcher call for the pitch he wants.

Finger signals have a way of being read easier by the opposition than by your own pitcher. We recommend that catchers flash finger signals as a dummy distraction, and that the actual sign be given by tapping the inside, say, of the right knee as the catcher goes into his crouch—for a fast ball; the left knee for the curve. (With finger signals flashed before and/or after simply to throw the opposition off.)

By the same token, there are very few pitchers in Little League who do not "tip" their curves in throwing them. Here again is a reason for managers to watch other teams' games as well as their own. Frequently he will pick off the catcher's signs. Just as frequently he will pick off some "tip" in the pitcher's motion or delivery that will top off the curve ball that way. He can then devise a spoken signal from the bench that will let his own hitters know what's coming next time they see that pitcher.

For that matter, the manager can call his own team's pitches from the bench—again, by means of some prearranged spoken signal. This takes a lot of application, and the catcher still should be using a dummy set of signals (without them, the other side is sooner or later going to get the idea that the pitch is being called from the bench, and once they realize that, it won't take them long to break the code).

What is being recommended here, in the way of signals, comes down to two things:

1. The fewer signals, the better.
2. Wherever the manager's mature judgment suggests to him that he is at least as well off calling the signals himself as leaving it to his pitcher and catcher, let him do the calling.

And the first of these alternatives is infinitely preferable, at the Little League level, to the second.

We have mentioned "setting up" a hitter through different kinds of pitches. The fact remains that where the pitch goes is more important than what kind of pitch it is. The batter who can't hit certain types of pitch is overshadowed, on the Little League plane, by the batter who has trouble not so much with the kind of pitch as with its *location*. All other things being equal, the predominant weakness among Little League batters is to be found in their inability to connect not so much in terms of *what* is pitched as in terms of *where* it is pitched.

Not only to such batters, but to all batters, the good pitcher (and a good catcher to go with him) will be *moving the ball*. There is arithmetic justice behind this principle. At most, the good pitcher in Little League will have three pitches. But there are *eight* strike zones! (And none of those eight includes the pitch across the heart of the plate.) There are inside high, inside middle, inside low, outside high, outside middle, outside low, center high, center low.

Obviously a pitcher needs control—but not pinpoint control—to take advantage of this.

As the count builds in the pitcher's favor, so does the advantage. It can get to the point of being overwhelmingly a psychological advantage. In Little League, where hitters are not skilled at protecting the plate, a pitcher with a count of no balls and two strikes ought never to "waste" the next pitch. We do not ask him to lay it across the middle for a strike, as he might do on a 3-and-0 count. We do ask him to tempt the hitter with a pitch slightly inside or outside (depending most of all on the hitter's known weakness). If the hitter lays off the pitch and it is called a ball, then the pitcher now comes back *with the same pitch.* Unless it is totally wide of the mark, this fourth pitch will so often strike out that hitter that it will begin to look like a hex. Psychologically, he is prepared for the pitcher to waste the third pitch on the 0-and-2 count, but there is nothing he can do when that same pitch comes back at him once again.

This, as noted above, does not require pinpoint control. If you do have a pitcher who can "thread the needle," then the opportunities multiply. Such a pitcher can make a batter "see the pattern." He will throw inside, outside, inside, and the batter will now subconsciously prepare himself for the outside pitch—and get it inside instead.

Unless the pitcher has fallen badly behind in the count, say at 2-and-0, his third and fourth pitches should be identical. This of course recommends a stringent pattern in itself, but it is remarkable how seldom the other side will detect it.

This technique—to make the third and fourth pitches the same—is the only piece of "pattern pitching" we recommend to Little Leaguers. It is simple enough for the pitchers to understand, complex enough for the opposition not to understand. As far as location is concerned, you cannot reliably begin to set a hitter up with your first pitch, because the first pitch is a no-cost pitch to the hitter. He can afford to be guessing all out, because the worst that can happen to him, if he fails to connect safely, will be a count of no balls and one strike, which leaves him very much alive.

The third-and-fourth pitch pattern, while it produces no absolute guarantees, makes sense from another standpoint: it is the only area in which the pitcher, depending on pattern, can be rewarded by a strikeout.

We have addressed no emphasis so far to the pitcher's stance, windup, and delivery motion because these are almost self-contained in the earlier recommendations for boys in playing catch. To review, the pitcher will want to take a relaxed, weight forward position, back toe on the pitching rubber, "throwing foot" a comfortable few inches in front. He bends his knees, both heels in contact with the ground. Then, shoulders forward, he goes into his "rocking chair" motion. At the front end of each rock, the weight transfers from the heels, and they come slightly up off the ground. At the end of the second or third rock, the hands come together, bare hand holding ball now making contact with glove. The hands now come up together behind the head and the body turns to a sideways presentation, with bent "throwing leg" in midair as the fingers, hidden in the gloved hand, take the desired grip on the ball.

How great a turn the body will take, how emphasized the pitcher's final kick, how great a stride as he pitches, all are matters for individual build and comfort. Wildness up or down, however, can frequently be regulated by altering the moment at which the player actually releases the ball. If he is coming in high with his pitches, he is probably releasing the ball too soon; if low, too late.

One dilemma for a manager, when it comes to sizing up his pitchers, is the discovery that some boys pitch better sidearm, or coming straight overhead or three-quarters but using too much arm and not enough body. When they are asked to use the "rocking chair" delivery, something seems to be lost in their ability to bring in the ball with maximum force and stuff. The temptation, particularly if they seem to be the best pitching talent available to the team, is extreme to let them pitch their way and not meddle with them.

Fortunately, this temptation arises only once in a while, for most pitchers find that the "rocking chair" not only improves their control but also adds to the impact of the delivered pitch. So at least a boy should be asked to try out the "rocking chair" style.

The occasional maverick who still throws a lot better using his own style should be allowed to do so, but with the admonition, both to him and to his manager, that if he relies more on his arm than on his body, he ought not to throw curve balls.

[6]

Defensive Strategy

The teaching of certain basic defensive plays will differ from the teaching of fundamentals in that some defensive skills should be common to the whole team, while others will pretty much depend on the position, or group of positions, that a specific boy is selected to play. If you have picked two or three youngsters to share the catching duties, there is no point in teaching the finer points of catching to the entire team. It can be boring, it consumes time, it produces no visible results, and in truth it is just as much a form of overcoaching as the teaching of ultrasophisticated tactics. A Little League youngster can absorb just so much, quantitatively as well as qualitatively.

Thus, while a good many of the recommendations contained in this chapter may seem like basic fundamentals, and even *be* basic fundamentals, the careful manager will hold up on beginning to teach them until he has begun to separate his fielders at least roughly into subgroups—first basemen, infielders, catchers, outfielders. This does not mean so much that basic techniques ought not to be explained to the entire team; but common sense suggests that only those boys more or less directly affected should put in any great amounts of time practicing them.

In this area, as in others, there will always be those plays that are taught differently to Little Leaguers than they are to more mature players. It is standard, for instance, and particularly so with runners on third or second, for the oncoming outfielder to be the one to catch the "Texas League" variety of fly ball; for any time there is a reasonable choice between outfielder coming in and infielder going out, the outfielder, with the play and the ball in front of him and the forward momentum for the throw, has all the better of it. In Little League, though, most of the talent is in the infield, and the infielder going back may be so much more reliable defensively than the outfielder coming in that it is he who should handle such balls on such occasions.

Many managers appoint a mature infielder (most often the shortstop, who is commonly both a good player and central to the action) to act as "field captain," and his shouted instructions, on all plays where more than one fielder has a shot at the ball, should be the final word.

Some teams seem to encounter repeated difficulty even deciding whether the shortstop or second baseman should be the man to cover second on an attempted steal. The basic rule, of course, is that the base should be covered by the man playing closest to it, and this will be the shortstop most of the time, because most frequently Little League defenses—again, unlike those at higher levels of play—are swung to the right, away from the hitter's power. Since most Little League hitters swing right-handed, against fast-ball pitching and (for many of them) even against medium-speed pitching, proper defensive alignment tends to the right side most of the time. (This does not mean the shortstop will handle any fewer chances. More of them, though, will be hit to his left than to his right.)

In a bunt situation, the shortstop should always be covering second whether the bunt occurs or not, for the second baseman must be going toward first base to cover there in place of the first baseman when the latter runs in to field the bunt.

On force plays at second base, the same rules for covering apply as on attempted steals except when the ball is hit to the first baseman (in which case it is always the shortstop who covers) or the third baseman (in which case it is always the second baseman who covers). This is because a fielder coming toward the direction of the throw can handle it far better than one arriving from approximately the same direction.

This is a good place to note, too, that in any situation where a throw between bases occurs when a base runner is in motion between those bases, the receiver should make sure he is on the same side of the base as the line of the throw. Otherwise, he will be setting up a target that will make the throw have to go "through" the runner. When the catcher fields a bunt, for instance, the first baseman must give him a target on the *fair* side of first base.

Boys expecting a tag play at a base should be on

the side or corner of the base that puts them closest to the throw and the oncoming runner both. (The actual position will change, of course, due to the angle of the approaching throw.) Sometimes, as in the case of a hit to left field which the batter is trying to stretch into a double, the baseman's back will be turned to the runner as the throw comes in. In such cases, the baseman should straddle the bag and give a very low target for the throw, so he can make the fastest possible sweep tag on a close play.

In every instance where the ball arrives before the runner, the waiting fielder should put the ball down at ground level on the runner's side of the base, and wait for him. Holding the ball higher and trying to tag down or out at the runner is a common and obviously bad mistake.

Fielders anticipating force throws, where no tag is necessary, should, as in tag plays, take their position closest to the angle of the approaching ball. Unlike tag plays, however, the other determinant of position—the oncoming runner—should find them farthest away from his line of travel, not closest to it. The ideal here is to avoid contact, rather than guarantee it.

Tag and force plays have in common the all-too-frequent blunder of trying to make the play without the ball. In tag plays, the fielder is moving his glove in for the tag before he really has possession of the ball; in force plays, we are treated to the sight of boys trying to keep one toe on the base instead of relinquishing the toehold in order to go catch the wild throw. A definite maxim for Little League managers to drum into their players is: *Get the ball first.*

Wild overthrows past first base are time and again the result of the first baseman's trying to maintain contact with the bag. The bad play at first base is the most damaging in Little League, probably, and not only because so many plays are made there. The real damage is more subtle, and it goes back to our earlier observation that the presence of base runners leads to extra errors. A ball that is dropped at second base on an attempted steal leaves a man on base, but he was on base before the play unfolded. Often at first base, though, the misplay means the difference between a bases-empty and runner-on situation.

In the major leagues, the first baseman covers the least ground and does the least throwing, and he got there to begin with because of his bat, not his glove. No one knows where elephants go to die, but in professional baseball they wind up at first base.

All too often in Little League, the same thing happens. It is not a question of age, but its Little League equivalents—clumsiness and overweight— seem tailored for first base.

While it is true enough in theory that lack of speed and fielding skills may do the least damage, in the case of a regular player, by putting him at first base, this truth exists only because of the greater skills and speed required at other positions.

This fact remains: the thoughtful manager will take as much time as necessary to work with his first baseman—more if needful than with a player at any other single position.

Essentially, this means working with his feet. To effect the maximum stretch, and the minimum entanglement with the runner or of his own feet and legs, the first baseman must concentrate on footwork.

Here, there are two widely differing schools of thought.

The old style, much in vogue a generation ago, was for the first baseman to take a position with both heels just in front of the base as he awaited the throw. If the throw was to his right, he would take a little hop step, anchoring the left foot on the corner of the bag and stretching with his right foot. And the opposite if the throw was to his left.

A more recent technique, also widely recommended (such as in a training film put out by the Los Angeles Dodgers), is for the first baseman to anchor with his "non-throwing" foot (*i.e.*, his left foot, if he is left-handed, his right if he is right-handed) and to do all his stretching with the other foot. In this manner, it is argued, the body can stretch in any direction in an unbroken line, since the arm with the glove and the leg doing the stretching are both on the same side.

In the case of a ball thrown straight at the first baseman, or not significantly off to either side, the two styles would of course pretty much blend into one. That is, the "hop step" stylist will anchor with his non-throwing foot and stretch out with the other.

The advantage to the old "hop step" style is that the boy gets maximum stretch and never winds up with his legs crossed.

The advantage to the modern style is that he does not have to search with a heel to make contact with the base, and generally the use of the same foot for all throws is far simpler to learn.

Bearing in mind that this is the Little League

102

level, this is one case where we would recommend the older and, perhaps, more complex style—the "hop step." It will take time to learn, admittedly, though once the player gets the hang of it he will have no problem locating the base with his heel—that part will come to him through practice, and once having learned it he will do it automatically.

The advantages for the Little Leaguer are several-fold. For one thing, as just mentioned, he will get a longer stretch on throws to his off side, and also he will not tangle up his legs.

Much more important, though, is the consideration that the newer style tends to "lock" or "freeze" the first baseman. The older style is much more free. Using the new technique, he will be prone to stretch off his base, with foot anchored, whether he can reach the throw or not. On throws to his left this can literally stretch him almost head on into the oncoming hitter, adding a threat of collision.

With the older "hop step" style, by contrast, the first baseman is by definition loose and un-committed—and he can do a lot more things as a result.

(An additional first-base notation is in order here. A little too frequently, sometimes deliberately because they think it's smart and no one will notice, first basemen in Little League are prone to take up a fielding position directly in the path of the runner between first and second. A good umpire will spot and put a stop to this at once, but Little League doesn't have that many good umpires. No manager should permit his first baseman to do this.)

No one, anywhere at any baseball level, has ever devised a foolproof scheme for telling a first base-man how far he should range to his right for a ground ball, and we have no secret tips to offer in this regard. If the pitcher is alert and capable and can cover first on hits to the right side, that is one thing. If the second baseman is good at going to his left, that is another thing. Of course, the baseman should know where his second baseman is playing, but even that is no standard rule to apply, because the speed at which the ground ball travels often sets its own rules (the first baseman typically playing considerably closer to the plate than the second baseman, who will be far back on the dirt, even on the outfield grass in some cases). In any event, the play should be worked on repeatedly in infield situation drills. The best we can offer is a general postulate that the better the second baseman proves to be at coming in fast and making the play on the slow-hit ball, the less the first baseman needs to range to his right, and the more often he can cover first himself.

Having somebody covering a base is, indeed, a prime and often-overlooked requisite in Little League play. *Go to a base—go to a base—go to a base.* The manager can make a litany out of it, and it will be a good thing if he does.

This can be the pitcher's job as much as anyone else's. He, and he alone, should be the cutoff man on throws from the outfield in Little League play. (We have already noted the singular physical characteristics and dimensions of Little League which make this proper.) For that reason—once again, unlike the situation in higher levels of base-ball—the pitcher should be as much a part of infield practice as the four infielders and the catcher.

In addition, the pitcher will field bunts more often than anyone else. He must cover first on ground balls to the right side. He must cover home on a wild pitch or passed ball with a man on third. He must back up third on throws to that base from right or center field. Even with just a man on first, he must cover third base on little fly balls hit back of third into short left field where both third baseman and shortstop are out in the outfield grass.

And he must remember—and all infielders must remember—that a play at one base does not end the play overall. A slide play at third, whether safe or out, does not mean there is now not a quick throw to second to get somebody else. With more than one runner in motion, boys should come up throwing, not waiting for the umpire's decision.

Backing up a throw applies to outfielders as well as infielders. Any time a potential overthrow will go into the outfield, that outfielder should be moving in advance to anticipate it.

The most confusion of all on backup plays occurs at second base. This is logical enough, since two men share the position.

On a throw from the catcher, the man who is not covering the base should try to be behind the man who is—and a good *10 feet* behind. It does no good for the second baseman to be picking the shortstop's pocket. He must have an intervening arc that will enable him to pick off the trajectory of a wild throw. Two men in the same place do no good at all. (The center fielder has a responsibility here too—he should be moving in toward the play whenever the throw to second can potentially over-carry into his territory.)

On base hits to right and left field, the backup formula is this:

Wherever possible, the "near" man should cover the base and the "far" man should back up the throw. On hits to left field, the near man is the shortstop, the far man the second baseman. On hits to right, the reverse is true.

If, however, the character of the hit takes the shortstop significantly away from second base, out toward left field, or the second baseman out toward right, then the other player—the far man —will cover the bag, and the backing up in case of an overthrow must be done by the more distant fielders—the first baseman on the throw from left, the third baseman on the throw from right. (In the latter instance, it may well devolve upon the pitcher to cover third base.)

This takes into consideration, of course, the fact that most Little League fields have outfield fences, and most of those outfield fences are close in. In the case of a poor-throwing outfielder, or a hit "up the alley" to left-center or right-center, or any long hit to any extra-deep field, the shortstop or second baseman—whichever is closer to the direction of the hit—becomes, perforce, a relay man, and *must* go well into the outfield.

Outfielders, in their turn, have special fielding functions all their own. On fly balls with a man on base who may advance after the catch, they should learn to make the catch by stationing themselves, wherever possible, behind the line of the ball's descent, then coming in to catch and throw. This puts added bodily momentum behind the throw. In many cases, they will charge ground balls hit through the infield. Their technique in these cases is the same as the infielder's—they come down with the "throwing" foot as they field the ball. A basic difference here, though, is that the knee of the other leg should make contact with the ground as they do so. This gives them a total block on the ball, which means that even if they don't field it cleanly, it will still not go through them. This is necessary because there are outfielders to back up infielders, but who backs up outfielders?

In Little League, outfielders' throws take on different characteristics from those seen at higher levels of play. For one thing, it is more common in Little League than anywhere else to find base runners who unthinkingly run on fly balls with fewer than two out. The double-play throw back to the base that the heedless runner leaves behind would be the best play in Little League—if only more *infielders* would remember to *go* to that base!

Time and again in Little League play, we have seen situations unfold with runners hopelessly off their bases—only to see the bases themselves uncovered.

If a relay man is involved, due to poor outfield arm or duration or direction of hit, then it is the outfielder's job to get the ball to him. (It is also the outfielder's job to assist, if not back up, another outfielder in every viable situation.)

But if, as most frequently happens, no relay man comes into the outfield, then the outfielder must be throwing to a base. There must be somebody at that base. It is as simple as that, and we only wish more teams would take it seriously.

In cutoff situations, the outfielder must throw directly to the cutoff man. Since it is the job of the cutoff man to line himself up between the outfielder and the farther target, this if anything helps produce accurate throwing.

The outfielder should not throw fly balls. Let

him instead keep his throw down—bounce it if necessary. In the professional Big Leagues, an outfielder who overthrows his cutoff man runs the risk that he may miss both runners. (We say "both," because if the situation does not give you a chance at more than one runner, then you need no cutoff man to begin with. A fly ball with none out and a man on third requires a throw to the plate after the catch. Forget about any cutoff man. There's only one runner to get.)

Of course, there is an added reason in Little League to keep throws low. In the professional leagues, overthrowing the cutoff man may mean you miss somebody else at another base. In Little League, an overthrow too often loses in time, because of its extra-high arc, what it gains in distance. So all players should be urged to keep their throws low. A low throw with as many as three bounces can get there faster than a high throw with no bounces at all.

Meanwhile, back in the infield, the pitcher, who is our cutoff man, must know whether to cut the throw off or let it ride through. Here finally, after all this discussion, we get to a point where Little League technique is far simpler than any other.

The basic fact is that the only cutoffs used in Little League will be on a throw to the plate, from any field, where there is an alternative chance: to get a runner at third, or to get the hitter who is trying either to stretch to second or to get back to first. (Other fielders, man your bases!)

On throws to third base from right or center field, the pitcher should be backing up third, not cutting off. Occasionally, on a throw to third from right or center, the shortstop will be in a position to cut it off, to prevent the hitter from picking up the extra base. But this will happen only when the second baseman is covering second at the time.

Appropriately, the next question is this: How does the pitcher, in the cutoff spot on the throw to the plate, know whether to cut it off or not?

This is the job of the catcher behind the pitcher. If he thinks he can get the man at the plate, he says: "Let it go!" If not, he says: "Cut it off!"

But that is not the way to teach it. Teach it so the cries are uttered not once but three times, in rapid succession: *"Let it go! Let it go! Let it go!"* or *"Cut it off! Cut it off! Cut it off!"* This leaves no doubt, and thus becomes infinitely preferable to the single utterance.

Little League base runners as a breed tend to think that any throw to get a runner ahead of them leaves themselves safe to move up. Perhaps the sharpest, yet most overlooked, play in all Little League is for the pitcher to cut off the throw to the plate and nail the hitter at second base. This by no means requires a situation where there is no reasonable chance to get the man at home. With a three-run lead in a late inning, you go for the man at second regardless of your chance at the man at home.

The score, the inning, and the number of outs each in its own way has as much to do with cutoff plays as the straight chance of nailing the farthermost runner. There are times when you give the opposition a run in trade for a far better chance of getting an out.

It is definitely our recommendation, in fact, that boys be trained in Little League to play for the sure out. Many are the times in professional baseball when the infield plays in for the play at the plate, but given Little League dimensions and the capabilities of the boys themselves, you will do this little if at all. Similarly, while it helps give boys the "feel" of force situations to say "Get two!" and have them practice double plays on ground balls during fielding drills, under game conditions it is far sounder to play for one out rather than two. Get either the "sure out," or the most advanced runner, depending on the situation and the score. (The "sure out" and the most advanced runner are often the same.) But don't have your third baseman give up the force play that he can get by touching third in order to try instead for the "around-the-horn" double play via second. We've stressed already that Little League field dimensions simply don't lend themsleves to the ground-ball double play.

In extreme situations—let's say, the home half of the sixth, or some extra, inning, with a man on third and less than two out, and the score tied— then of course you have to play the infield in. Unless your pitcher is known for his control, you can't set up a force by walking the hitters. But, short of extreme circumstances like that, play for the sure out. This particularly applies to first basemen who can get the hitter by tagging first after picking up his ground ball. If they can get him out that way, it should take an extraordinary situation to have them try for an out anywhere else.

In recommending this procedure, we may be giving up a double play or two along the way. But over a season we will get more outs.

There can be two logical exceptions to this general rule. With bases loaded and the factor of

110

an even reasonably close score, and less than two out, the play should be on the most advanced runner—the throw to the plate—even though a force play at another base is somewhat handier. And with two out, again even though a force elsewhere may be more inviting, the throw should usually go to first base, because the runner arriving there—*i.e.*, the hitter—gets the worst start, thus should be slowest to arrive.

These points, especially the last one, are subject to variation, through speed and direction of hit and position of fielder. If the fielder with a force play at second or third is traveling toward that base when he fields the ball, and can easily beat the runner to the bag *without having to throw*—or, at second base, has an easy and short toss to a fielder already covering the bag (again, one that can easily beat the runner)—then obviously the nearer play is preferable to the longer throw to first. So perhaps the idea can best be stated this way: with a choice of force situation and two out, when in doubt go to first.

The unassisted force play at third base has a couple of interesting ramifications in Little League —here again, because of the frequent overshift of the defense to the right. For weak hitters, in bunt situations, and generally to pick up the slowly hit ground ball to the left side, the third baseman will quite often be not only pulled a good way off his base, but positioned in on the infield grass, with the base path behind him. This makes covering third a difficult task (we've seen runners on second steal third and actually get there before the third baseman does).

For this reason, among others, we tend to discourage the "extra" play at third base, like the pick-off throw from the catcher after a pitch. With a man on third, the third baseman certainly should go to his base, or at least toward it, after each pitch (with a man on second too, for that matter). But even a good-throwing catcher will have to wait for his third baseman to reach the bag; in most cases, with the majority of hitters being right-handed, the catcher in throwing to third must throw "through" the hitter; and the consequences of an overthrow mean a run scored against you. The ability of the shortstop to function as a backup man at third is not high in Little League, because so frequently the shortstop is not only playing so deep but likely to be swung toward second base.

In individual batter cases where the defense is not overshifted to the right, there is of course more access to plays at third base.

We are talking, though, about the most common variety of defensive alignment in Little League. Again here, a difference should be noted between Little League and regulation style of play. There are standard instances at higher levels of play where the *third* baseman acts as cutoff man. In Little League, this must always be left to the pitcher. The third baseman must go to his base (or at least toward it) after every pitch. The only exception will be when he is in actual pursuit of a batted ball.

Occasionally, both shortstop and third baseman will go out onto the outfield grass, often along the foul line, for a pop fly. In such cases, the pitcher must cover third base.

This factor of relocation and replacement has

especial meaning in Little League where the distance between players is comparatively so small. And nowhere is it seen so graphically as in the case of running down a man between bases.

This play—known to kids since time began as being "in a pickle"—is one that even professional major leaguers find difficult to execute properly. For youngsters, though, it is a "fun" play, and Little Leaguers will readily practice it as much as half an hour at a time, though they will much more quickly lose interest in some simpler defensive exercise.

One of the things that make the "pickle" enjoyable to practice is that, by rotating fielders and runners, the coach can put the whole squad into competitive action, so the drill need have no idle onlookers.

Four fielders, two at each base, are needed to execute a correct rundown format. Each base is covered by an "initial man" and a "backup man," as follows:

If the rundown is between	The initial man is	The backup man is
First and Second	First Baseman *Shortstop	Pitcher *Second Baseman
Second and Third	*Second Baseman Third Baseman	*Shortstop Pitcher
Third and Home	Third Baseman Catcher	Shortstop Pitcher

* Shortstop and second baseman are interchangeable in these instances, depending largely on who is closest to second to begin with.

Three basic principles apply to the correct execution of any rundown play. They are:

1. Both bases *must be covered* at all times.
2. Chase the runner *back* toward the base he started from. That way, even if he escapes the pickle, no advance is likely to occur. This means that in chasing the runner back toward the base he came from, the fielder will chase him as far as possible, throwing the ball only when holding it any longer would permit the runner to regain his base before the ball gets there. Conversely, in chasing him forward toward the next base, the fielder will wait only till the runner is at a point where, if he now changes his mind and tries to get back to the base he started from, the return throw will be there in time to get him.
3. The ball should be thrown to, and caught by, only the boy standing on the base. No intervening fielder should ever try to touch a thrown ball during a rundown.

If these principles are followed, virtually the only circumstances in which the runner can get out of his predicament will be if there is a fumble, a bad throw, or that occasional horrifying moment when the fielder throws north while the runner is headed south.

Let us take a rundown between third and home, started, let's say, by the catcher. He will be at home plate as the play starts and the third baseman will be just reaching his base, if not already on it. The catcher now starts running toward third with the ball, chasing the runner back and using jerky cocked-arm threatening motions with the ball as he runs. (If at any point he actually tricks the runner into thinking a throw will be made, so that the runner changes direction and starts for home, then the catcher has a made-to-order tag put-out.)

Once the runner is within 20 feet of third base, the catcher throws to the third baseman. The catcher now veers to his left, into foul territory, and circles quickly back toward home plate, which is now being covered by his backup man, the pitcher.

At this point the third baseman has the ball. He starts chasing the runner back toward home, using the same deceptive arm motions, but permits the runner to advance no more than halfway home before throwing the ball to the pitcher now covering there.

The pitcher now does exactly what the catcher did before him. The third baseman meanwhile veers to his right, into foul territory, and circles quickly back toward third base, which is now being covered by his backup man, the shortstop.

And so the weave pattern evolves. In the next sequence, if there is one, the catcher and third baseman will once again anchor home and third respectively, while the pitcher and shortstop enact the "circle weave."

Note that the ball, when thrown, always goes all the way to the base. And there must always be somebody there to catch it. It is a great temptation for boys who do not have the ball to come off their bases in the direction of the oncoming runner. (This is true not only in rundown plays, but in other situations. A sad and frequent sight, and not just in Little League, is that of a catcher, say, who comes up the line toward third while awaiting a throw. The ball is thrown to him there, but the runner goes past him in the process. If the catcher stays at home plate, the burden of extra time and distance is on the runner—which is where it should be. The only excuse for a fielder's leaving his base before getting the ball is if he sees that the throw is coming in off target. For the fielder deliberately to set himself, as a target in advance, not on his base but up the base path toward the approaching runner is, as we have said, a great temptation. It is tempting because psychologically the boy wants the ball as soon as possible. But if he stays on his base, the ball will get there to him more safely— at least it travels faster than the runner.)

In the rundown play, there is an added temptation, along these same lines, to throw the ball to some intervening fielder between the bases. This can be executed well by professionals with 90 feet between bases, but the rule in Little League should be that the ball is thrown only to the man on the base.

When all is said and done, it can be surprising how well Little Leaguers handle this play, mainly because their enthusiasm for learning it makes up for the sophistication that comes with experience. Sometimes the enthusiasm becomes excessive; particularly with more than one runner on base, outfielders like to get in on the act too, and with more than one runner on base—assuming the basic rundown is against the most advanced runner and handled by infielders only—there's no reason why they shouldn't. In practice sessions, however, one rundown at a time is plenty for boys of Little League age, and the drills should be restricted to infielders only. Under game conditions, blundering runners and happy accidents sometimes can get two outs instead of one, but that is far too complex a matter to teach in advance.

With men on first and third, and the right combination of score and inning, the defensive team can frequently *force* a rundown situation. In such cases, it is so automatic for the man on first to take off for second on the first pitch that a quick throw from the catcher—apparently aimed at second base but actually aimed at, and cut off by, the pitcher—can trap the runner off third. Of course it is the third baseman's job to get to his base instantly. The pitcher's first move is to look there, and if he sees the runner trying to scramble back and knows that he has a play, he throws at once to third. If the runner instead is committed all out to coming home, the pitcher throws to the catcher. If the runner "hangs himself up," waiting to see what the pitcher will do, the pitcher should keep the ball and run directly at the runner. Oftentimes, he will make the tag himself. If the runner breaks in either direction, the pitcher then throws the ball to the fielder on the base the runner broke toward, and once again, if the runner now changes direction, the rundown sequence gets under way.

This play naturally has the disadvantage of conceding the steal of second to the runner who was on first, but in the majority of first-and-third situations, unless the offensive team is trailing by a sizable score, the defense must pretty much concede that steal anyway.

One exception to that automatic concession in the first-and-third situation comes when two are out. In such a situation, given a good-throwing catcher who has caught the pitch cleanly, then in almost all cases early in the game, and in most cases late in the game except for a tied or one-run-margin score, there is no reason for the catcher not to throw down to second for the put-out which will end the inning. (An extremely clever base runner on first can "hang himself up" in such cases so the man on third has time to get home before the out is made, but such shrewd running is practically never encountered in Little League.)

With a runner on second, a catcher should occasionally at least bluff a throw to second base after the pitch, to get it into runners' heads that too much of a lead may hurt them. And every team should have a catcher—an alert first baseman too—who will sometimes try the pick-off play at first base after a pitch.

One extremely rewarding pick-off play comes when the first baseman is charging in for the expected bunt. The second baseman, whose job it is to cover first in such cases, comes in from behind the runner and covers anyway, even if the batter does not make contact with the ball. The runner, lured into an extra-long lead because the first baseman is not covering, is now nailed by the throw to the second baseman.

As a rule, we do not recommend "pitchouts"—pitches thrown deliberately wide of the plate to facilitate a catcher's throw to a base. When all is said and done, boys *cannot* take the kinds of lead in Little League that they do at higher baseball levels, and at the Little League level a catcher who is good enough to get his man with a pitchout is probably good enough to get him without one. And pitchers' control being what it is in Little League, it is perhaps just as well not to look for extra ways to throw a non-strike.

On that same subject, but for different reasons, the intentional base on balls is also of dubious merit in Little League play. The intentional walk, in regulation baseball, often has at least the partial purpose of setting up the double play, but the ground-ball double play happens so infrequently in Little League that all it means at that level is another base runner.

Managers do well to remember also that Little League games last only six innings, and strategy tailored to the nine-inning game is something that does not apply in every case to a game only two thirds as long. The intentional base on balls has the automatic effect of moving the entire enemy batting order up one notch. They have only so many big hitters, and one should think twice before going to extra lengths to improve their chances of coming to bat an extra time.

In all cases you will want your pitching, when facing a big hitter, to work if not to his weakness then at least away from his strength, and in some particularly threatening situations this can result in the "unintentional intentional" base on balls.

But the only time we would counsel the all-out deliberate pass would be with two out late in the game, and then only (a) if bases are empty, or (b) if first base is open and the tying and/or winning or go-ahead runs are already on base. Even then, the manager will want to bear in mind the ability of the hitter next due up.

Under certain circumstances, the recommendation against the intentional base on balls can be relaxed to this extent: that once the count has reached the 3-ball point, with the pitcher behind at 3-and-0 or 3-and-1, it may be the most discreet thing for the pitcher to throw the fourth ball deliberately wide rather than have to fight too hard for two or three strikes in a row.

Generally speaking, pitchers of Little League age do not have sufficient control to throw "off pitches" when behind in the count, or when the count is 3-and-2. Little League hitters take far more pitches than they swing at, and at the risk of letting them sense what pitch is coming, the base on balls is not worth the gamble of trying to make them go for a breaking ball on 3-and-2.

The percentage in having a lefthander or a right-hander pitch to specific hitters can figure into the manager's thinking, but since most hitters are right-handed and few Little League bullpens can provide strong pitching without jeopardizing eligibility for further work that week, it is mostly an idle exercise.

All this spells out yet another reason why the key spot on any Little League team, game in and game out, is that of the catcher. Among other things, an alert catcher will be the first to notice what pitch happens to be working against a certain hitter in a given game. (Less than half the time will this be the pitcher's doing—instead, it is batters who change more from game to game, uncon-sciously using a different stance or swing.)

And, although the shortstop may be field cap-tain, it is the catcher who has the entire game in front of him, and who, on short hits or bunts, calls out what base should be thrown to.

Four physical tips for catchers may be in order here:

    1. Never place a knee on the ground. It makes throwing almost impossible.

    2. Never just drop the mask when getting rid

of it. Instead, cast it a good distance away, into foul territory away from the direction of the play itself. The dropped mask is too easy to stumble over.

3. Whenever possible, make tags with two hands, rather than with bare hand holding ball. (The more common gloved-hand tag is of course not possible for a catcher.)

4. When handling a fast-ball pitcher, use a thin sponge in the mitt.

The sponge mentioned just above is one of two props that are valuable in Little League play. Another is an ordinary piece of burnt cork. This may be used to paint a layer of charcoal under the eyes of boys who may be fielding into the sun. Unlike most professional fields, few Little League layouts are planned with the points of the compass in mind, and most Little League games are played in late daytime, typically with a 6 P.M. starting time, when the sun is at its lowest and therefore can hamper fielders the most, via direct glare. In such cases sunglasses are useless, but charcoal can be of some help.

The physical borders of a Little League field itself may play their own part in altering defensive technique. Take the case of a single to right field with a man on first. We have already recommended that the pitcher must back up the third baseman on such plays. But if your field has a fence very close to third base, as some fields do, then no backup man is needed, and in that case the pitcher here could act as a cutoff man instead, with the possibility of getting the hitter trying to advance to second on the throw to third.

Once in a while—on a hit to right field with a

man on first where the second baseman covers second and the shortstop backs him up—the direction of the throw will mechanically turn the shortstop into a "free" cutoff man; that is, he will be lined up with the throw to third base. A right fielder with a strong arm can use his shortstop as a cutoff man as he throws the ball to third. There are not very many right fielders with strong arms in Little League, and so this is probably not worth working on. It is a play whose basic ingredients don't unfold that often anyway.

All outfield throws should be directed toward a base, and should of course be made immediately. The game is in the infield. Outfielders who hold the ball or tend to run in with it should be told that a bad throw is better than no throw.

An opposite problem is that of the outfielder who can and does throw—but always in the general direction of home plate, whether or not there is a play there, or, when there is a play, whether or not the man going home is, in view of the score and inning, the most important man to try to get.

Shouted instruction from the field and bench, and repeated "situation" drills in practice, are the best antidotes to this. Outfielders should be taught never to throw *behind* a runner—i.e., to a base the runner has already reached or rounded. (The only exception here is of course the caught fly ball where the runner is in motion instead of going back to tag up—then the throw back to the base he has left can produce the double play.) In fact, unless there is an obvious play on an obvious man at third or home, all balls to the outfield in Little League should probably be returned to second base. Not only is it the most logical place most of the time, but it gives the outfielder the shortest throw.

Little League generally does not produce good defensive outfielders—with a real and not altogether infrequent exception in center field, which should be manned whenever possible by a regular who is good with glove and arm. The reason overall is of course that within his roster limit, the manager will have only so many boys with good defensive talent, and they are needed in the infield.

(The talent range is so limited in Little League, in fact, that the one thing professionals never do— have their pitchers catch pop flies—becomes, in Little League, one of the most common of plays. It is not unusual in Little League to see the pitcher —what with ground balls, bunts, and pop-ups, not to mention his role as cutoff man—accept a maximum number of fielding chances in a game.)

It should be remembered of Little League outfielders too that, as a breed, they come in better than they go back, and in playing a given hitter, any outfielder whose ability is in doubt should station himself a good couple of strides (at least) farther back of what otherwise would be classified as his "normal" depth for that batsman.

Position, alertness, and proper deployment all can be taught. But the skills that will be helped by these factors need nevertheless to develop on their own, and here there is no substitute for exposure and experience. This is true of all defensive positions. Meanwhile, it is the wise manager who will settle for the basics on defense, and trust that the complexities will be served later.

Many plays, in truth, depend most on a "sense" or "feel." Example: While going for the sure out or the most advanced runner—and in so doing, sometimes not going for the double play, which is so hard to get—boys should nevertheless bear in mind, whenever possible, the prevention of unnecessary advance. A runner in a non-force situation, at third or second, should always be "threatened" back to his base by a player fielding a ground ball before the fielder throws to first. This threatening look involves mostly the pitcher, third baseman or shortstop with a man on second, or the third baseman or pitcher with a man on third. If the fielder is behind the runner—such as the first baseman with a man on second—there is not too much point in giving a threatening look to a runner who isn't looking at you. But once in a while he will look at you. Any fielder who has time to give that look and still get his man at first should certainly do so.

[7]

Offensive Strategy

No strategy or tactics within a manager's power, for the sake of getting the best out of his offense in any given game, can equal his ability to draw up a proper batting order. Too often this element is neglected or just plain misunderstood, and boys are chosen because they are "natural cleanup men" or "natural leadoff men."

A properly devised batting order in Little League will take a different approach, because of three factors that apply to Little League only:

1. Most Little League hitters are not good hitters.

2. In Little League, the manager has an obligation to use *all* his players in a game as often as possible.

3. Little League games last six innings, not nine.

As a general rule in Little League, your best

hitter should bat third, your second-best hitter should bat fourth, your third-best hitter should bat second. This presents the greatest chance for them to have runners on base ahead of them, for we are given in advance two innings: the first and second—one third of the entire game—in which it is extremely unlikely that any of these three hitters will be a leadoff man. By placing this strength high in the order, it also maximizes the chances that your power will come to bat an extra time.

What is also at work in that kind of scheme is the factor of *protection*. It is not difficult for Little League defenses to understand that if a very good hitter is to be followed in the batting order by a very bad hitter, that very good hitter is not going to see too many good pitches. The defense will pitch around him—sometimes issue the intentional or the "unintentional intentional" base on balls—and take its chances with the next man. This may sound sophisticated, but it is a technique seen in Little League, and if opposing clubs don't think of it the first couple of times, they'll come to learn it.

Even managers who appreciate the value of a protective batting order often let things get away from them as they start to put substitutes into the game. Or they draw up a nine-man batting order, in which everybody protects everybody else, only to forget that once the game is under way there is no such thing as a nine-man batting order. Thus not only should hitter No. 9 protect hitter No. 8, but hitter No. 1 should protect hitter No. 9.

It's a useful thing for a manager to rate the hitters on his team, on a scale perhaps that might look like this:

A—Very good
B—Good
C—Fair
D—Poor
E—Very bad

It has to be understood that on a typical roster the C, D, and E youngsters will outnumber the A and B youngsters by a good two to one.

In drawing up his batting order, the manager will then wherever possible follow these two precepts:

1. Never bat more than two D or E boys in succession.
2. Never follow a hitter with another hitter more than one step lower on the scale. That is, an A hitter should be followed by at least a B hitter, not a C, D, or E. The C hitter should be followed by at least a D hitter, but not an E.

Remember also that this philosophy of protection should extend to treating the No. 1 hitter in the order as the man following ("protecting") the No. 9 hitter—with this interesting exception: Some managers have hit on the happy expedient, particularly when they are the home team, of putting a couple of young substitutes in the starting lineup, rather than trying to get them in later in the game, and the leadoff spot is a particularly good place to put one of these less talented or younger boys. It has extra meaning when you are the home team, because it means these boys can start the game by playing at least an inning (particularly if you are using a good pitcher) in the outfield—especially left field if you have a fast pitcher. Use such a boy in the field in the top of the first and at bat leading off the home half of the inning, and he can now proudly say that he not only got into the game—but got in the *starting lineup!* Depending on several factors, including how the game is going, the manager then can remove him from the lineup upon, or even before, his second turn at bat. (This thus is the exception to the need of your No. 1 hitter in the lineup that starts the game to "protect" the No. 9 hitter, since that protection will become the job of the boy who takes the No. 1 hitter's place second time around.)

It also can be mentioned that if your team gets off to a good-sized lead at the beginning, the young boy who got to start can be kept in the game, and under such conditions we can forget the "protection" rule his second time at bat. In general, most if not all of your younger or less talented players will gladly accept in trade the guarantee of an occasional starting assignment for the far more uncertain possibility that they might get to play a longer stretch of time later in the game—if they get to play at all.

We have noted that the C, D, and E hitters will strongly outnumber the A and B hitters. Sometimes the D and E hitters will actually outnumber the A, B, and C hitters. But when the manager has enough A and B hitters so he can not only bat them second, third and fourth in the lineup but still have one or two left over, he ought to withstand the temptation to lump them all together. That might be all right in a key game or a championship game, but there is a lot to be said for spotting a good hitter as far down as seventh in the batting order—and a lot also to be said for letting him sit out the first few innings once in a while, then putting him in the game at the most appropriate moment. This latter device gives a Little League team a strength most Little League teams seldom make use of: a strong bench. Early in the 1967 National League season, the Giants clinched two consecutive victories against the Dodgers because Willie Mays was on the bench. In each case, the Dodgers pitched to good hitters with first base open, because to issue the intentional pass under such circumstances would have brought Mays up as a pinch hitter with bases loaded. And in each case the hitter, who was being pitched to instead of walked, delivered the key safety.

One final additional reason in favor of using the less talented or younger boy at the start of the game is that the manager need not, for the sake of getting the boy into the contest, have to worry about changing his lineup at a later and more critical point. This takes on especial meaning in the case of extra-inning games. The manager who, whenever possible, uses his less talented or younger boys in the early going, will go into extra innings with his best lineup on the field. The only way the opposite-minded manager can bring about that result is to use a minimum of substitutes if any. The more games a manager wins, the better baseball job he is probably doing. The more boys he can get into those games, the better overall job he is probably doing. A manager with a really good team can afford of course to start a lineup composed mostly of second-stringers from time to time. But the manager with the average team will want to think seriously about that combination of tactics which will best combine the chances for boys to play with chances for winning.

The strategy for advancing runners is second

only to the science of drawing up a batting order, when it comes to developing offensive results. Here again there is a walloping difference between Little League and the higher levels of baseball. In the professional major leagues, for example, a hitter who can get a runner from second to third with none out by hitting a ground ball to the right side is a hitter who's done his job. But in Little League, a boy who can control his bat sufficiently to hit the grounder to the right side is too good a hitter to be wasted on the resultant out at first base. Similarly, while he was with the Dodgers, Maury Wills by definition *had* to be their leadoff man. Here was a case of a player not only who could bunt and run, but whose speed was dependent on the *absence* of a slower runner on base just ahead of him. Also, he played for a club whose pitching kept the score close, and Wills, for all his brilliance as a base stealer, was a creature of the scoreboard: put his team down four runs in the score, and he wasn't going anywhere.

All this sort of thing simply does not apply to Little League. A boy who is a fast runner and a good bunter (especially a left-handed hitter) is welcome as a leadoff man, but his gifts can be equally valuable farther down in the lineup.

As for stolen bases, most of them are the catcher's doing, not the runner's. At higher levels of the game, leads are taken on the pitcher, and if he throws a change-up a base can be stolen just on account of the extra time it takes the ball to reach the catcher. But this sort of thing is against the rules in Little League, and the result is that most stolen bases aren't even close. Either the catcher drops the ball and the base is stolen, or he holds

it and—assuming he has any kind of arm at all—
the runner is out. The close plays on steals in Little League result therefore not so much in a race
against time as from a bad throw on a pitch that
was caught cleanly or from an extra-good throw
on a pitch that was dropped.

Because of the inordinate frequency of passed
balls or wild pitches in Little League, boys have a
way of getting from first to second, and not infrequently from second to third, whether the "steal
sign" is on or not. We do not know in advance
whether a given pitch will be caught or dropped.
But we do know in advance how good the other
team's catcher is at throwing the ball. As a working rule, therefore, the steal sign should be put on
with respect to the catcher's known ability as a
thrower, more than with respect to the situation of
the moment.

Another thing to remember is the infrequent occurrence of the ground-ball double play in Little
League. Thus there is practically no need in Little
League to steal second to wipe out the threat of a
double play. As for hit-and-run or the runners going on the 3-and-2 pitch, these moves are prohibited by Little League rules and so play no part in
offensive thinking.

Finally, with a good hitter at bat, we would
rather give him a runner on first base whom he can
advance or drive home than risk the out at second.

The real fact of the matter comes down to this:
In professional major-league baseball, a man on
second is in scoring position, a man on first is not.
In Little League, *any* base runner is in scoring position. (Or, if he isn't, chances are he soon will
be.) A Little League base runner who is compara-

tively slow but very alert will move up far more frequently than one who is comparatively fast but not keyed to take advantage of sudden opportunity. To state the obvious, it is also better to have a runner who is fast and alert than one who is slow and alert, but speed per se should not be the main regulating factor in a manager's decision to try to steal a base.

The sacrifice bunt has much the same significance—or, rather, lack of significance—as the steal, in Little League play. Once again, the fear of the ground-ball double play is almost nonexistent in Little League. Once again, there is no point in deliberately giving up an out. And once again, the fielders' capabilities need to be judged ahead of the hitter's. Given a poor-fielding pitcher and third baseman (but not necessarily first baseman—bunts to the right side can wind up in the unassisted tag along the line), even bad bunts will work, and plays which would never be tried in the professional Big Leagues—like the bunt with the bases loaded—can profitably be employed, especially when the hitter is less effective when swinging away. The bunt with a man on third in a non-force situation is an almost sure guarantee of a run, particularly when the catcher fields it—or at least gives chase—and the throw is then made to first (which leaves nobody covering the plate).

Every bunt should be for a base hit, regardless of whether the hitter squares away beforehand, thus leaving himself flat-footed and tipping the defense to his intention. One of the great plays in Little League occurs when the power hitter bunts with two out and the winning run on third. Psychologically, it has the effect of paralyzing the defense. But once again in this connection, we would discourage bunts to the right side. The first baseman can make his own play on the ball, but the catcher, pitcher, or third baseman has got to put the ball in the air, and at the Little League level this extra invitation to error should be exploited by the offense.

In discouraging the stolen base and the simple *sacrifice* bunt, we are of course cutting down on the number of signals a team will use. For a man on first, the steal sign should be relayed to him by the first-base coach. All other signs should come from the bench.

Signals in general are a problem in Little League. For the boys' sake they have to be simple. Yet when they are simple enough for the boys, they become simple enough for the other team to read.

One answer is to give the hitter his instructions before he goes up to bat. This, however, is of minimum value because any such instruction is most commonly applicable only to the first pitch the hitter sees.

There is, nevertheless, a marvelously simple way to handle the business of signals to the hitter. The manager calls to the boy by his first name, and as the boy looks the manager wipes his hand across his shirt, or tips his cap, or whatever. No matter what the situation is, the manager always gives the same sign. This is bound to confuse the opposition, because they cannot see the connection between the signal and the different things that happen in response to it.

The stunt is that as the boy looks at the manager, he is also looking at another player on the bench who, on instruction from the manager, is actually giving the real signal. The manager himself is going through one consistent and standard dummy motions that means nothing.

Some Little League teams like to use "answer signs"—that is, the hitter uses a signal to show that he has received and understands the sign that was flashed from the bench. There is no actual purpose in this at the Little League level. Answer signs are used at the higher levels of baseball play to guarantee that a base runner will not be hung up off his base because the hitter failed to get the sign. But because Little League runners can take no leads off the pitcher, their chances of being hung up are no worse if they don't know what's coming than if they do. It's nice if they do pick up the sign for their own information, but under playing conditions it doesn't make enough difference to be worth the added complication.

There are only four "signal" situations in Little League: steal, bunt, take the pitch, and "call it off" —that last meaning that the order in effect on the previous pitch has now been canceled.

We have already in these pages recommended a minimum of "take" and "steal" signs. In six innings' play, the "take" sign is too often abused. We would use it most frequently on a count of 3-and-0; much less frequently on a count of 3-and-1; hardly at all on 2-and-0. But that policy presupposes fairly good hitters. In the case of an overanxious hitter, an obviously wild pitcher, and a player with a propensity to chase bad pitches, we have an entirely separate reason for using the "take" sign, even on the first pitch. Again here, we have a totally different set of circumstances from those applying to higher levels of the game. Here, we are putting the "take" on not because of the situation, but to calm our hitter and give him a chance to get ahead in the count.

The wise manager in Little League will not incline to order his hitters not to swing at what may be the best pitch they'll see all game, and this can apply, with a top hitter, even in the 3-and-0 situation. As a rule, the better the hitter, the less he should be controlled from the bench. As another rule, the hitters' various capabilities should decide whether the "take" sign is given, as much if not more than the situation at any given moment.

There can be extreme circumstances—two runners on base in a late inning of a close game, 3-and-0 or 3-and-1 on a good hitter with an even better hitter next due up—where the "take" makes a great deal of sense. The "take" has to be most effective, of course, when the count has reached three balls, because then the next pitch can produce a walk and another base runner. Even so, it is silly to order a good hitter, who figures to come up only three times a game, to lay off a fat pitch. And so restraint from the bench—the "non-sign" —is often the best sign of all.

Ironically, but perhaps fittingly, it is quite often the manager who overdoes signs the most who neglects the greatest signal opportunity of all. Of all curve-ball pitchers in Little League 50 percent depend on obvious signs from the catcher and 75 percent give away their delivery beforehand. A predetermined shout from the sidelines ("Come on, now!" or "All right!"—something as simple as that) can tip the hitter that the curve is coming. It is remarkable how often the curve ball can be picked up by the other team's bench—and, surprisingly, it will often be a player, rather than a manager or coach, who does pick it up. Pitchers not gifted in hiding the curve grip, or catchers who display their signals too openly, are sitting ducks for an alert opposition.

We have already mentioned specific opportunities for runners to advance—the third baseman out of position with a man on second, the catcher moving out of position with a man on third. Some prearranged shout from the bench can help here too. Using the runner's first name—"All right, Harry!"—can be as good a code as any, to realert the runner that he has the chance to move up on a mishandled pitch.

Such prearranged signals can readily enough be separated from a continuous chatter from the bench (which serves its own purposes). It is a bad and quite needless mistake for a manager, coach, or players on the bench to slacken off in their cries of encouragement simply because the game seems out of reach. Encouragement should, if anything, sound louder when the team seems hopelessly behind.

It is expected also that not only hitters but also base runners will be given both encouragement and guidance from the bench. Situational reminders, particularly score, number of outs, and the presence of a runner at the next base, should constantly flow toward your base runners. In this case, there is a very good "answer sign" that can be employed. You call to the runner. He looks at you and nods his head.

Speaking of simple techniques, there is one that is almost frighteningly simple—yet it works time and again. Given the situation of a runner on third base and a hitter who receives a base on balls, let the hitter not just trot to first base, but instead, when about halfway there, break into an all-out run, round the bag, and head for second.

What does the defense do now? If they try to get the runner between first and second, the man on third scores in the meantime. If they let the hitter have second base, then the base on balls has become worth a two-base hit. At the Little League level of awareness, the offense can pull this stunt time and again without the defense being able to set against it. The truth is that the most frequent result of this play is not just that the hitter reaches second, not just that the man on third scores, but that *both* of these things happen!

[8]

Umpiring:
A Case of Neglect

The manager's job in Little League—not by himself, but in concert with the other managers in his league—needs in most cases to extend to teaching umpires as well as players. Good umpiring not only produces the best baseball, but is by far the most important single weapon in controlling high feelings, fan reactions, and all of the side squabbles that leave a bad taste in everyone's mouth. We assert that it is the manager's job to work with umpires, because there is no one else to do it.

Umpires should be older than Little League age; but the uncertainty of adult schedules, or the presence of an umpire who wouldn't even be there if he weren't some player's father, means that day-in, day-out umpiring by adults is in most cases neither possible nor desirable.

Baseball-playing high schoolers therefore form the best pool of umpiring talent for most Little Leagues. Typically, in a "major league" game, there will be a plate umpire and a base umpire, who will make a dollar or two each for working a game.

These boys should be met with and worked with, not only on more than one occasion before the season begins, but, if possible, once or twice during the season as well.

It is no one's fault, but umpiring in Little League is too often a sheer case of neglect, an unwanted stepchild of the Little League program, so to speak. This can only have undesirable results, and a little attention on the managers' part will go a long way toward setting this key situation right.

First off, umpires should *know their rule book!* They should, in fact, carry the book with them at all times, and not be afraid to consult with each other any time one is in a better position to see a play than the man whose call it is, or any time there is doubt as to a rule.

Balls and strikes, "foul" and "fair," "safe" and "out" should be called in a loud voice, with visible arm motions for everything except a ball, in which case the absence of any arm motion becomes a signal in itself.

Umpiring by explanation is not to be desired. Say "Ball two," don't say "Too high." Even worse than umpiring by explanation is the case of Charley Even-up, the umpire who, having made a miscall, decides to give the next close one to the other team in order to balance things off. If an umpire's judgment is consistently bad, get another umpire. But a second bad call is no way to wipe out one bad call.

Balls and strikes, "foul" and "fair," "safe" and "out" should be called not only assertively but as quickly as possible. All pitches should be called at once. Sometimes *foul, fair, safe,* or *out* must await the full outcome.

Plate umpires should crouch directly behind, and as close as possible to, the catcher, and should view the pitch from just over the catcher's "inside" shoulder—the shoulder closest to the batter. Calling pitches "over the top" or over the "outside" shoulder are both bad practices. "Over the top" causes the umpire to miss the low pitch; over the "outside" shoulder tempts him to confuse the inside corner with how close to, or far from, the plate the batter himself is standing.

The base umpire should never take a position on the infield grass. He does it in regulation baseball, yes, but as we noted at the outset, the square footage of the regulation diamond is more than twice the square footage in Little League. The added presence of the umpire inside the base paths serves only to overcrowd the scene.

With no one on base or with a man on third base only, the base umpire takes his position on the outfield grass along the right-field foul line, and runs in toward first base, or over toward second, on any play developing there. In such cases, he is also the best judge of whether a ball along the right-field foul line is fair or foul. In all other cases, and in every case of a ball along the base line on the infield side of first or third, the plate umpire is the judge of fair or foul.

With a man on first, or with men on first, first and third, first and second, second, or bases loaded, the base umpire stations himself on the outfield grass about midway between first and second.

The plate umpire calls all plays at first and third.

These are typical alignments in a typical two-umpire situation. Little League, unfortunately, is more difficult for two umpires to handle than any higher level of play, because the base umpire must be alert to a boy's leaving his base too soon *at every base*. (The plate umpire has to call the pitch and cannot be looking elsewhere.)

Finally, umpires *must bear down on every play.* There is nothing wrong with an umpire's failing to call a play if he can honestly say "I didn't see it"—but in order to say that honestly, he must have been preoccupied with a preceding development. Inattention by itself is no excuse. Unfortunately, it is the most common cause of disputes on the field.

The worst foes of Little League are, in this sense, the people in the stands. They have a rooting interest, or most of them wouldn't be there. And inevitably they will jeer the call that goes against their team.

Yet an occasional bad judgment call—if it is given authoritatively, quickly, and clearly—is not what stirs up the fans. The umpire who is in doubt, or obviously doesn't know his rules, or isn't paying attention, or gets in the way of a play or is otherwise flagrantly out of position—this is the man who generates (too often all unwittingly) three-quarters of the friction in the stands.

The worst, and a most frequent, occurrence of bad umpiring involves the umpire who is miscalling the pitches because he is positioned too far back of the catcher. This is the umpire who guarantees that not only the stands, but the players themselves, will be "on" him, and it is sometimes difficult for a manager to calm down, say, a pitcher who knows he has thrown a strike when not just bad judgment, but impossible positioning, has brought the umpire to calling it a ball.

In this respect, umpires psychologically behave

like catchers—they tend to want to move *back* from the pitch so as not to be hit by the errant delivery.

The truth is that in the umpire's case, just as in the catcher's case, the closer the umpire gets to the pitch, the less chance he has of getting hit by a stray ball. The close-up umpire has, in fact, the safest position of all, for the closer he is to the catcher, the more his guarantee that the ball, if it does go awry either from pitch or from foul tip, will, if it hits anybody, hit the catcher and not him.

It is our conviction that a good portion of the publicized ills of Little League could be avoided by an umpire who works a close and confident balls-and-strikes situation, and who shouts out his verdict on each pitch so no doubt can take hold.

And over and beyond that specific, the better the umpiring, the better the game, the better-behaved the players, and—to gain a goal that no manager on his own can teach—the more orderly the adults in the stands. One can never say how much any given individual will respect authority or even competence. But the *absence* of either quality is an open invitation to bring out the worst in the spectators, as well as in the players, managers, and coaches.

A sizable amount of anti-Little League sentiment can be traced to bad control of games. Control is measured by good umpiring. Good umpiring, at the practical level, is the responsibility of the team managers. This therefore comes very much under the purview of this handbook, because any manager who has a choice between an extra practice session with his players and a chance to sit down with the umpires will as a matter of straight common sense choose the umpires.